A RASPBERRY SEED
UNDER GOD'S DENTURE

William M. Beahm

A RASPBERRY SEED UNDER GOD'S DENTURE

The Wisdom and Wit of William McKinley Beahm
Missionary, Preacher, Educator

by Earle W. Fike, Jr.

THE BRETHREN PRESS, ELGIN, ILLINOIS

Library of Congress Cataloging in Publication Data
Fike, Earle W.   1930-
    A raspberry seed under God's denture.

    1. Beahm, William McKinley, 1896-   I. Beahm,
William McKinley, 1896-   II. Title.
BX7843.B4F53   286'.5   79-14074
ISBN O-87178-733-4

TO JEAN

who laughs easily and beautifully
who is not afraid to cry
who helps to make life whole
who is my most special person
and who has solemnly promised that
no book dedication will change her.

ACKNOWLEDGEMENTS

Special appreciation is due:

to Esther Eisenbise Beahm, who gave permission and encouragement and shared her memories;

to Harriet Beahm Kaylor and her husband, Earl, who gave helpful advice on specific information and materials, and who graciously allowed me to soundly wreck their dining room for several days while I rummaged through letters, papers and files;

to Anna Beahm Mow, with whom I've had a constant love affair ever since she laughed her way into my life as a seminary teacher in the early fifties, who since then has given spiritual and personal support for my ministry, and who gave good counsel and insight for this work;

to Paul and Mary Robinson, who gave a night's lodging and several hours on two different days to remember and laugh and marvel at seminary experiences while Paul was president and William was dean;

to Carol Sherbondy, who learned to know William only second-hand as she typed much of the material from dictated tapes, assorted scraps of paper and "quick before we forget . . ." short-hand notes; and who acknowledged the material others shared;

to Jim Lynch for a paper with biographical and library information;

to Fred Swartz for his helpful counsel as editor;

to all of the following, who wrote, called, or in some way shared a memory:

William P. Albright
Shantilal P. Bhagat
Harold Z. Bomberger
Ralph D. Bowman
Walter D. Bowman
Charles L. Boyer
Dale W. Brown
Clyde Carter
Esther K. Crouse
Merle Crouse
Donald F. Durnbaugh
John and Jessie May Eller
Chalmer Faw
Darlene M. Garwick
Wayne F. Geisert
H. Lamar Gibble
Ellis G. Guthrie
Chester I. Harley
Graybill Hershey
Grace Hollinger
Fred Hollingshead
Wilbur R. Hoover
Roger Ingold
Stewart B. Kauffman
J. Wilburn Lewallen
J. Henry Long
Joseph M. Mason
James McKinnell

Matthew M. Meyer
John C. Middlekauff
Baxter Mow
Mildred F. Mundy
Hubert R. Newcomer
Galen B. Ogden
Hazel Peters
Carroll Petry
Harry Reeves
Jacob F. Replogle
Henry H. Rist III
Jimmy R. Ross
Leona Z. Row
Donald E. Rowe
Celesta Wine Shippey
Paul F. Shrider
Don Stern
Goldie W. Baugher Sterner
Owen G. Stultz
John Thomas, Sr.
Nancy Trout
Robert Wagoner
L. John Weaver
Ronald K. Wine
Jesse H. Ziegler
Phil and Margaret Zinn
Edward C. Zook
Cleda Zunkel

TABLE OF CONTENTS

FOREWORD

William was my only brother. Father said he had five daughters and each one of them had a brother. He was a very welcome little boy. Later Mother told Sara, two years older, that she said about the new baby, "Kiss him whole lot, little brother." He was always appreciated by his younger sisters, also.

As I recall, William always had a certain timidity; but with it a consuming curiosity about everything, especially how things worked. His timidity may have been due partly to his physical condition as a child. On his first birthday Father wrote in his diary, "Willie is one year old. Dear boy! He is small but pert. He has had hardship." (They had almost lost him that first year.) I remember that Mother often spoke with concern about his health as he grew older.

But William's curiosity took over in the summers he spent at Grandpa Bucher's farm in Pennsylvania. Even at eight he knew enough about the steam engine to make a suggestion to the bewildered specialists who had come to make needed repairs. His suggestion worked! He also had to know about that big sack in the barn with the corncob stuck in a hole near the bottom. He pulled the cob out and watched entranced as the fine clover seeds slowly oozed out. Of course, Grandpa came along just then and, without a word, took William and dipped him in the rainbarrel at the corner of the barn.

William's potential weakness from his shyness was overcome by his evergrowing faith in a loving Heavenly Father and his acceptance of the available grace of God. Like Paul, his weakness became his strength. His curiosity led him into a continuous quest for an understanding of man's relationship to God and to the practical theological explanation of that relationship. I felt that he became truly humble because he knew that his natural self-abasement was conquered by the grace of God.

Three weeks before he died I had a whole day with him all alone, while Esther had needed tasks to care for elsewhere. He was in great suffering, but he talked of his loving concern for his beloved Esther and, most of all, about the meaning of death. Without fear, he looked forward to being with the Lord but still wondered what the passing would be like.

I am so glad that Earle Fike has written my brother's biography. William always appreciated Earle so much and I know Earle felt the same way. Earle has the same gift of words. God bless his story.

Anna B. Mow
Roanoke, Va.

INTRODUCTION

Every person is unique and special. Some seem more so. William McKinley Beahm was a "more so" person. I want you to meet him. If you already know him, then this is a chance to remember and perhaps to expand your knowing.

This work is not intended as a biography; a careful chronological cataloguing of historical material; a review of contributions or assessments of William's life. It is a portrait of the man, a good bit of it in his own written and spoken words. Some is from the collected folklore of many who loved and enjoyed him. It somehow seemed second best to write words about William if there was some way to allow his words to provide the basic brushwork for his own portrait. So the only words about him are a few as introduction to each chapter; some here at the beginning, and a few at the end of the book.

William Beahm was a much loved and respected man in the Church of the Brethren. He was a churchman of the highest order. His teaching of those preparing for ministry for 25 years, his service as secretary of the denomination's Annual Conference, his two terms on the General Board of the Church of the Brethren, and his two elections to the highest elected office in the denomination, the moderator, put him on the inside of the ministry and mission of the church. Good words to characterize his churchmanship would be wise and judicious. In meetings small or large, hot or boring, his contributions were eagerly heard. Often on issues that seemed hopelessly snarled or polarized, he would begin, "I have two or three observations to make. . . " and he would proceed to offer such carefully thought out judgments that helpful agreement often resulted.

William was loved as a teacher. He was a good one. In his years at Bethany Theological Seminary, the winds of doctrine blew around him; sometimes in tornado like whirlwinds, sometimes in subtle seductive breezes. While he was conversant with new directions in theology and was willing to dialogue in depth on new trends, he managed to stand firm in traditional theology. This book does not give due credit to his stature as a theologian. To fill in that part of the portrait, the reader needs to spend time with William's major written work, *Studies in Christian Belief,* The Brethren Press, 1958.

William was loved for his memory. Rather than "nobody knows my name," hundreds of people throughout the Church of the Brethren could rightly say, "someone knows my middle name." When William met you, he noticed things about you, physical characteristics like eyes and bone structure, which he catalogued with all the family lineage information he could learn. Then, with some kind of mental paper clip, he attached it all to your geography and name and filed it in a remarkable fastidious memory. The next time he met you he could call you by name; first, middle and last. Somehow it never seemed "show off." It made you feel special.

His concern about names led him to study the meanings of many names. That concern was also reflected in his own preference about his name. He did not like to be called by shortened versions. He liked to be called "William."

William was loved for his wisdom and wit and humor. People often spoke of him as being wry or dry. The story goes that, while William was a student at Manchester College, Otho Winger, a man William greatly admired, told him that he would be more effective and appreciated if he didn't laugh so much at his own humor. William resolved then and there to reduce his own participation in what he said. His niece, Lois Mow, once said to her mother, "Uncle William says funny things, but he's so solemn. Is it all right to laugh?"

My memory makes no connection between William and a guffaw—it doesn't fit. An outright laugh was extremely rare and effusive. A hearty chuckle was permissible, but leaned on the extravagant. Yet, the lines of his face were pleasant, his wrinkles turned the right way, and the twinkle in his eye betrayed his enjoyment of word play and humor.

William's wit was both immediate and planned. He was a connoisseur of words and idioms, and he poured over his treasures like a coin collector or a rock hound. If something struck his fancy, he stored it away, squirrel like, to be brought forth in some cold, barren discussion that needed the medicine of mirth. Additionally, he had the real humorist's sense of timing. He was not intrusive. He did not seek to be heard. But when he spoke, people listened. And he refused to play the "I heard one better than that" game. Some of his word play appears in these writings, where he spells words phonetically rather than correctly.

Despite William's calm, sure, deliberate way, there was in his character a combination of insecurity, shyness, and feelings of unworthiness. This trait may have contributed to his profound sense of the grace of God. But it is also why he fretted so over decisions and found some hard to make. And it may be one reason why he found it so difficult to write a book. Like many an artist, he was concerned that the form and content would somehow jeopardize the message. He was such a careful workman that he wanted each word right. I've wondered if the book was not harder for him because he made the decision that in "Studies in Christian Belief" it was not "all right to laugh."

William and his lifelong companion, Esther Eisenbise Beahm had a close and warm relationship. Early in their letters it is already clear that Esther's energy, ambition, and strength, her confidence in William, her encouragment to him would be a lifelong moderating influence on some of his own insecurities. Home and family were very important to William. Home was a place of love, a place of acceptance, a place of strength and support.

Home was also a place where William liked to putter and tinker. He fixed things. Owning their first home in Villa Park, Illinois late in their life together was special to William and Esther, and projects like the back yard patio constructed of "stolen" bricks were pure delight to him.

He wrote notes on scraps of paper, bulletins, anything that was handy. On a church bulletin from Whitefish Bay Community church, dated 1955, I found the diagrammed solution to a puzzle on how to get three missionaries and three cannibals across the river in one boat without jeopardizing the lives of any of them. And on the back of a funeral expression of appreciation was written a list of the ten worst dressed movie stars, with explanations for their rankings, which he had hurriedly copied while watching a TV show.

My own pilgrimage with William began in a little interview room at Bridgewater College as he worked with me on pre-enrollment for Bethany Seminary. From 1951-54 he was my teacher. In 1957 I became pastor of the First Church of the Brethren in Chicago, a block and a half from the seminary. For five years I was pastor to William and Esther. Two of those years he was moderator and elder of the congregation and for two of the five years we served together on the General Board of the denomination. Few young pastors are blessed with such strong support and such probing of ideas and concepts. He was teacher and counselor. He was also friend.

A pinch of laughter gives credence to credo. Humor is a grace. Dr. Bevel Jones says, "Humor and faith are cousins; both deal with the incongruities of life. The aim of life is wholeness, and faith without humor is incomplete." Reinhold Niebuhr defines humor as the prelude to faith, and laughter as the beginning of prayer. William was a whole man. And his profoundness and depth was somehow authenticated by his humor, as for instance his original definition for *sin*—"a raspberry seed under God's denture."

So, this book is a collection of the things William wrote and said. Even the chapter headings are his words. Much of the writing shared here has never been public. It was written to family. Through their graciousness, I was given freedom to go through his letters and papers. I found no skeletons—nothing there that surprised me. There were words and feelings that enlarged and enriched my understanding of him, and added to an already cherished portrait.

William McKinley Beahm. One of God's special persons. I loved him. I hope you enjoy him.

Earle W. Fike, Jr.

CHAPTER ONE

"Dear Hoamfoax . . ."

"A child is born, a son. . . " Dated Nov. 4, 1896, the note is from the diary of I.N.H. Beahm, William's father. We begin this portrait of a man with some words about his early life from other persons: William's father; his sister, Anna Beahm Mow; and a childhood cousin and friend, Esther Crouse. There is a story about his early life shared by his uncle, Rufus Bucher; and two childhood stories which in later life William shared about himself.

William joked about how often he moved as a child. His early addresses included Tazewell, Brentsville, Nokesville, and Trevilion, all in Virginia; Lordsburg, California; and Elizabethtown and Mechanic Grove, Pennsylvania. He was baptized January 20, 1910 in the Nokesville Church of the Brethren and in 1915 graduated from the Academy of Hebron Seminary in Nokesville.

The letter to "Hoamfoax" carries an undercurrent of some of the anger William felt at his itinerant father for leaving the burden of the family on his mother and him. In a November 10, 1918 letter (Chapter Two) he refers to a growing reconciliation between him and his father.

The chapter ends with letters he wrote home, the earliest in 1910 at the age of 14, one at age 17 in which he needs a suit, and the last at the age of 21 from Akron, Ohio where he still needs a suit, but finally has one ordered with "preacher coat and vest."

From the Diary of I.N.H. Beahm

Nov. 4, 1896—12:05 P.M. a child is born—a son. I'm glad. We wanted a boy but made no calculations expecting to be satisfied with boy or girl.

Nov. 8, 1896—Babe and Mary doing well but he does not nurse enough.

April 7, 1906—Go with William on his way to George Buchers. Aunt Lea meets him to go the rest of the way. Sorry to be separated from son.

Sat. July 21, 1906—Took train to George Buchers to see William. Found him with a broken arm. He's doing well.

* * *

From his sister, Anna Beahm Mow

"When we lived at Elizabethtown, Pa. on Willowsprings Farm (1900-1909) it was William's business to care for the barn and cow."

"When we were young, we would have been punished more for saying 'ain't' than for telling a lie."

"When we lived in Virginia, we raised tomatoes and lived in a 100 year old house with 7 fireplaces and 24 oak trees. Carrie was a black girl that helped us. When she was working hard, sometimes William would say, 'look at her blushing.' William got his first bicycle there but there was no place to ride it."

"When William was eight, grandfather found him sitting alone in the big red barn. There was a full bag hanging there and at the bottom was a corn cob stuffed into a hole in the bag. The bag was filled with clover seed—very precious. William had pulled the cob out and was sitting there transfixed, watching the seed run out in a pile on the floor. Grandpa Bucher didn't say anything. He put the cob back in the hole and picked William up, carried him around the corner of the barn to a rain barrel and dunked him. When William told about it later, he said of course it was three times."

"Quipping was a part of our everyday life."

* * *

From Mrs. Esther K. Crouse, Queen Ann, Md.

"William stayed at our home two summers. He was there in 1910 when my uncle threshed wheat by steam engine. He urged my brother and me to follow him as he crawled through the wheatthresher blower pipe one evening. We were to crawl all the way through and tumble out onto the new straw stack. I got panicky half way through and backed out."

"There were no dull moments when William was at our house. My Dad was building a new granary with a cupola on the roof. It was almost finished when William encouraged us one at a time to get into a bushel measure to which he had attached a rope. He put the rope over a rafter and pulled us up so we could see out of the cupola. It was fun."

* * *

Story told by Rufus Bucher, William's Uncle

(William did not like to be called by nicknames, but Rufus could call him "Willy" and it was okay.)

Willy had a broken arm about the age of 10. He was at his uncle's where they were threshing grain. It was a new threshing machine, and like most new farm equipment, needed much coaxing to get it going. Belts needed to be tightened, sprockets and chains needed to be adjusted. The morning was spent trying to get the machine to work with no success.

When the men returned from lunch, they began again to survey and tinker with the machine. Little Willy came over to one of the men and said, "Why don't you take this belt right here, pull it off and twist it." The men were desperate, so they did it. And the machine worked. Rufus looked at Little Willy and said, "How did you know that would fix the problem?" Willy's reply, "I've been sitting here reading the instructions which came with the machine."

* * *

In a class discussion on the second coming, William told of an early experience. His father, I.N.H. Beahm, had prepared to leave home one mid-summer to hold a two-week revival in a distant congregation. He left with the understanding that William would hoe the corn. William decided that the corn could easily be hoed in one week, so he spent the first week playing, swimming, and fishing. The same kind of reasoning kept him out of the field one day at a time during the next week. As the end of the second week drew near, he realized he could not finish hoeing the corn before his father arrived, so the plan was to wait until Monday morning when he saw his father coming down the road, and begin to hoe vigorously. But his father didn't come home from the direction William expected!

* * *

William shared that at a very early age, "I used to walk backward through the fresh plowed corn field to the swimming hole, so if I.N.H. discovered my tracks, they would be leading away from the creek rather than toward it."

* * *

Handwritten letter dated 1910

Denton, Md.
July 10, '10

Dear Mother and all,

I would have written a whole lot sooner, but did not get at it. Aunt Annie took Bucher along to church this morning. It is raining this evening. I saw Albert Seese's wife in church last Sunday and Susie Seese. We got done thrashing yesterday noon. Uncle Milton had two acres in winter oats and thrashed 142 bushels from it. He had 80 acres in wheat and thrashed 1543 bushels from it. Bernard stepped on a rusty nail this evening. It hurt him bad.

We have two colored hands. One of these hands is Frank, and John the others name. He has one called Abe that helps him arrange for harvest. Frank and I hauled the water for the traction engine all the time we were thrashing. It took us about a day and a half to thrash. Aaron Reber thrashed for us. Did Esther get my ball from Ward Garber yet, if she didn't tell her to get it and if she did, I wish you would send it to me by mail if it does not cost too much. Aunt

Deborah is my Sunday School teacher. I hoed the garden on the fourth of July.

July 12, 1910

We cut spring oats yesterday morning and then Uncle Milton and I took a calf to Ridgely and I got my hair cut for 15¢. We have a calf about two weeks old now. We have 3 steers, 1 bull, 64 cows, and 5 heifers. We have 3 mules, 5 horses and 1 colt about two years old. I helped Aunt Annie to wash this morning. Brother Imler and Bro. Brumbaugh are the only preachers we have at Ridgely. Uncle Milton sold his other place to Harry Holsinger. I guess that is all I have to say this time,

William

P. S. How is the wood pile?

* * *

Hand written letter dated "Home 6/9/13"

Dear Pop,

Mr. Sheldon has Jack in the mower today. He wants him tomorrow, also. I'll let him have him. The oats has grown up and filled out very well during the rainy season. I replanted the corn. The grass is growing. I did not ask for $5.00 for bicycle repairs but for $5.00 to get a summer suit. Sam Brexton wants $11.55. We have about the best stand of corn around here. That's all.

William

* * *

Handwritten letter dated 1916

807 Coburn St.
Akron, Ohio
Oct. 22, 1916
4:10 P.M.

Dear Hoamfoax,

Here we are again. I am still rooming at the German lady's house with Earl Weaver but expect to move about Wed. I was going to Bro. Border's but now I am going to the Parsonage. That's pretty good, eh? I am getting acquainted with quite a few people. Over last Sat. and Sun. I went out to Springfield congregation (about 6 miles east) to an all-day meetin' and love feast in the evening. They served dinner at the church in the genuine old fashioned Pa. Dutch style. I enjoyed the apple butter bread immensely as well as the free plain Dutch spirit.

I went along home with one Irvin Schrock who has lived in Pasadena California for quite a while. His wife was a Miss Kurtz who knew Katie Hoffer out there. They are a fine couple. *Young* middle aged folks. That's the kind I like.

Brubaker's are that kind too. I'll be glad to get over there to room. And they askt me to room there! I have been working 2 weeks now and have made about $26.00 but won't get any until next Friday. What I has saved up at Sterling is nearly gone. I owe Perry Williams $50 and could have had that paid two weeks ago if I'd have staid at Sterling. But with $10 carfare and 4 wks living expenses in Akron and about $6 worth of clothes and no pay surely eats up the coin.

I will take me three or four weeks to pay Perry yet and then I'll have to keep enough to live on two week so you can imagine whar I is. And I need a suit too which I figured on getting about the middle of ~~Sept.~~ December. So if I do that I'll not be able to amass any great fortune until the first of the year.

What did you figure on? For me to pay you my savings this winter and then you lend me coin for school next fall? That will be alright if I can get to saving soon enough to keep you from starving.

You know that all the money making training and opportunity I ever got at home would poorly fit me for paying my way thru school and my time besides. If I'd have been started in some line of work instead of spending 4 or 5 summers on the farm I might be better able to make some more coin but as it is I'll be able to save only enough in 15 months to pay my debts, get some clothes, and about $350 to go to college on. And by the time I pay about $275 or $300 time money out of that there won't be much left. So you see I *will* be careful who gets my time money. If I were going to school for commercial advantages the ? would be different but since it is for mission work I can't afford to go in debt.

Now what is my duty? to you? to the church? to God? You have no means of support. Should I work to keep the family together? Somebody must. Somebody hasn't. I would like to. But is that my highest calling right now? If it is I want to be willing to do it. Or can that be done by some who aren't preparing for mission work? I am ready to do my duty.

Monday 11 A.M.

I had to go last evening to practice 2 quartets for the Young People's Temperance program last evening. It lasted from 6:40 til 9:00. Fine program.

Next Sunday they will have a Rally Day in S.S. They want to have 300 present. They run about 180 to 200.

I haven't written to Wilby yet but want to soon. I hardly know what to say. Did you know I got a letter from Chester? Well I did. I got one from Martha Senger too. A nice one. I sent her a picture.

I must write to Anna yet. We ought to be able to get a family letter started again soon so it wouldn't tax you so much. You may write to one of the girls next if you prefer and I will await my turn.

Speaking about my time money, I don't feel as much like I ought to pay for my time as I ought to help you and the younger girls to make a living. I'd be willing to let my time money come out of my inheritance which will probably be the case for the timebeing if I borrow for school next fall. Well, we'll wait and see. I'll let you have all I can spare as soon as I can spare it.

I must go to dinner and then take a nap so I can work tonight. So I'll stop.

William

* * *

Letter dated "Akron, O. January 5, 1917" to Mrs. Mary Beahm

I got youall's letter on Wednesday eve. I got another two since I wrote last. Wed. eve I worked from 6:00 p.m. till 6:30 a.m. I made $5.98. I made $3.77½ last night in seven hours. It takes effort, however. I hope to reach $4.00 in a week or two.

On Monday I went to a bunch of cousins who are keeping house for dinner. Some feed, too! We fooled around and talked in the p.m. Then we had supper. Fine time. We are having cottage prayer meetings in Akron this week. On Tuesday it was here. I led. They are conducting a city-wide evangelistic campaign from Christmas till Easter. Last Sunday they had a "go to church tonight" invitation canvass. I helpt divide and assign our territory.

I am a church janitor now—$10.00 per mo.

I got a $15.00 money order the other day, but haven't had a chance to write yet. I appreciate my Christmas money very much, but I think I'll send it back. Then there'll be no transportation charges. C? Therefore . . . enclosed please find check and money order for $16.00. That'll make $46.00 so far. Will $200 be about right for the whole business? I want to pay that and make enough for 1½ years of college besides. Big Job. Hard work. Satisfaction guaranteed. I can send between $10.00 and $15.00 every week if all goes well. But I want to get a suit in several weeks. That'll cut a little.

* * *

From "Akron O. Jan. 21, 1917"

Dear Mother and family,

I got your last letters all right. Was going to send you some coin on Tuesday, but you said wait until January 30. And I was going to write you Friday eve, but you said at the beginning of the week. So here I am. I got a letter from Anna and Sarah. I answered them and am sending them on. I sent Anna $10.00. How much will you want at the end of January? I would like to pay the $200 as soon as possible; but if it isn't safe, I'll send as you need it. I ordered me a suit last evening. It cost $30.00. But it's a suit. My roomate got one for $15.00, and it is worth it. I may have gone a little steep, but I'd have to pay $25.00 for a good blue serge and this is $15.00 better. It's silk wool fabric. Preacher coat and vest. I got a $2.00 hat but hardly have the nerve to wear it. I am so used to a cap. It makes me feel like a man.

The other Sunday a tall, redhaired gentleman walked up to me and said, "Schaeffer." I said, "I thought so, this is Beahm. Don't you remember when we took the Melton girls home from Shumake's and got lost on the way back?" "Oh, William Beahm!"

CHAPTER TWO

"Fan the Embers . . . "

"It is singular that my happiest days have been since Feb. 7, 1916." So William wrote in 1920, suggesting that the time of his original meeting with Esther Eisenbise came during 1916 when he was attending Bethany Bible School and involved in the Student Volunteer Movement for Foreign Missions.

The chapter begins with letters dated 1917 from Akron, Ohio, where William was "earning coin" by working at the Goodyear Tire Company. July 1917, he was ordained to the ministry at the Akron Church of the Brethren, and that fall entered Manchester College. William and Esther both received the A.B. degree from Manchester, Esther in 1918 and William in 1920, and were both enrolled in Bethany Bible School from 1920 through 1922, receiving B.D. degrees in the spring of 1922. The day before Christmas, 1921, they were married.

"Fan the Embers . . . " includes excerpts from William's letters to Esther during this period. They are filled with word games, expressions of deepening love, periods of anguish and decision. They give testimony to the real strength and support which he felt in Esther, feelings which he carried throughout his life.

The chapter concludes with a letter to his mother written after their marriage and while he was traveling with the Student Volunteer Movement. There is also the complete text of a handwritten speech from college days on the "Origin and Significance of Arbor Day." Words are underlined as they were in the original text. His fascination *with words is clear in this early writing. One is grateful that as he matured, he tempered this ability rather than letting it loose on us unchecked!*

From William to Esther, July 18, 1917, Akron, O.

Dear Esther,

I did not get your letter until today, and woke up to read it. I must say I don't regret the loss of sleep a bit. I appreciate and value your interest and concern regarding the greater responsibilities of life. I am sure you will be a help rather than a hindrance. You are now, and have been "4 a'that and a'that." I am glad for the "God Speed, too."

The preacher wants me to make my debut before I leave here. Several have spoken to him about it. I hardly feel like that is God's speed. It seems to me there would be too much curiosity in the audience. I am not afraid of discouraging remarks as much as I'd be of flattery (without discretion and rational judgment.) I'd rather start where they don't know it's the first time, and then after I am in school, I'll be in a better position to do the necessary studying and thinking than I am now. If I come back next summer, I'll be willing to give them a message. I'll be older and not so inexperienced and the curiosity phase shall have worn away. Here's the idea—I don't like to preach with the idea of learning to preach, but I want to feel that the people need a message and I can give it. There is one preacher Cross here and a preacher Murray. If it is not curiosity, why don't they ask them to preach sometimes? Maybe I am finnicky, but I hardly expect to submit to their rush. I believe I could meet their approval, but that isn't what I want to preach for. So it goes. . . .

But, on the other hand, I must confess I'd hate more for our association to break now than I would have before I went to Hoffmans. And I've really held that association in its proper place better than I expected. I like the idea of confusing certain public opinion, too. So, all in all, I can give you liberty without reluctance because I believe it will do us all good. I am trusting you as you have trusted me.

On Sunday I went to the country for dinner with a bunch of boys and half a bunch of girls. Had a nice time and came back with the boys. I played tennis three hours last Saturday with Mr. Hiller. Expect to play next Saturday. On the 28th is our Sunday School outing. I am to give a humorous speech.

I didn't work last Thursday and Friday nights. The power was out of wack. I read, "The Printer of Udell's" on Friday and shed a lot of tears. I enjoyed the book. I read it before. I think I'll go to visit Miss Porter soon and hear my music. Perhaps Saturday night. I like her but I'm glad she's much older than I am.

May the Lord broaden us enuf for development, but keep us narrow enuf for strength and safety. Sincerely,

William

* * *

From Akron, Ohio, June 3, 1918

My dear Esther,

I didn't think until this morning that you will leave Chicago before this gets there but I don't know where else to send it so I'll take a chance on sending it to the old home. I hope you'll get it before you get the next one. I am sure you'll forgive my thoughtlessness.

Last Friday I helped to fill the war chest for YMCA and Red Cross by allowing the company to take $1.50 out of my wages every month. Very few men give voluntary contributions, but they get it anyhow. There are no slackers in the Good Year because they fire those who don't contribute. So there! I am glad to help, however, but I'd rather give to the Student Friendship Fund because that will have a $500,000 missionary budget on it this fall.

And then I joined the Good Year Relief Association and I don't have less faith in God because of it. I still have my life policy in my mother's favor and I couldn't be impartial by giving it to any of my sisters and _____ otherwise _____? That reminds me: What do you mean by, "I feel so good, but _____?" Is it your lung or your heart? . . . .

We went to C.W. on time. And I talked ten minutes on "only Love Can Appreciate Christ." I was nervous, slightly, but after I was up, I never felt more calm before. I was glad for that. I am telling you these things because you are one big reason it is easier for me to do them . . .

When I come home Saturday, I got your second letter. (I am still counting them) and I felt like a renewed soul I was.

* * *

From 28 South Martha, U.S.A., June 20, 1918

My dear Pioneeress:

Were you ever up in an airship? Henry Adrian, the Burbank man was and the motor stopped and he nearly ran into the earth. So he said last night. I heard him at the Chataugua. I am going tonight to hear Ford the electrical wizard. . . .

How can you send 20 pages for 2¢ when it costs me 6¢ to send that much to Chicago? I must have used BASO 4 paper and you are pretty far away after all. I was looking for Alta the other day and was surprised to learn of your extreme westerliness. It's great to be at different places at once though, isn't it? But say, if I am there as you say, and I know, and you are here as I say, and you know, where are we? . . . .

Brubaker gave some high points of the conference and then preached about the Holy Spirit. I believe that people who like a sermon mostly noise are few. Brubaker hammered the pulpit and yelled, "it is not *force* that will conquor the world." Isn't that funny? Then he continued to yell about Peter's gentleness after conversion. It tickled me, but I pitied him. Then he spoke of Peter's education at the feet of Gamaliel and about his action in the Philippi jail. Such blunders will hurt the size of a congregation.

Co. Bain gave his lecture tonight and his power is old fashioned, new spirited, eloquent optimism. In his appeal for "see America first" he said many people went to Europe six times who never saw Niagara Falls or the Mrs. Sippi River and who never heard of our western states where folks with weak constitutions could live on by-laws. He said in Utah, the center of a family Bible looks like a hotel register. He said he saw a man once who was so lazy that it rested him to look at him, etc. etc. . . .

I believe I had better send this soon. I have really enjoyed writing and don't want to keep you waiting so long next time. I appreciate your interest in me; and if I can be worthy of it all, I shall have neared my ideals.

Determinedly,
Your William

* * *

From Grand Rapids, Mich., July 24, 1918

My dear Blossoming Ideal,

I was truly and happily surprised last evening. Kathy Wondergem stopped in here and said, "Did you get your letter?" I said, "No," and went along with her home and there was a fat, healthy one from my dearest inspirer. I read it through, and througher, and felt like a bigger man which I was.

* * *

Long letter from Manchester College, Nov. 10, 1918

My Loved Fairy Queen,

The war isn't over yet tonight that I know of. But I am not putting any deferred classification on my love for you. But, my dear girl, I believe it is almost necessary for folks to live together to be really happy. I am afraid that I am developing a mood that letters don't reach, but still it isn't long till Christmas. Maybe my interest in my studies doesn't enter my letters as much as the reports of Akron doings did. Or maybe it is because I am wearing a tie and feel a slight disapproval from some folks. Or maybe it's because I've decided not to go to Clear Creek. Or perhaps it's because vacation dampened my morale and I have a lot to do now. Maybe it's because I haven't engaged very seriously in religious services for a long time. Or maybe Church History has relatively disparaged some of my former religious beliefs. Or maybe I've been liberal on some ideas that I've lost some valuable convictions. Or maybe I am just plainly lonesome—my own sympathetic sweetheart, there is something wrong with me or I would't start letters twice before being satisfied with myself and I wouldn't write, "M.C., Sunday P.M." and wait 5 or 10 minutes before beginning the letter proper (or improper).

On my way back from Michigan I wrote the letter to you, on the train, and I hadn't made as good financially as I needed to for the best self-confidence (and yet I worked all the fit days) and didn't get the letter to you on time then, and that spoiled your plans. And I gave you due credit for feeling disappointed about that. And the next letter, last Tuesday, was two days late and unfair to you and you probably didn't get the one from Huntingdon until it was overdo. However, it was written with noticeable relative freedom. I have prayed a little too prosaically and hurridly to be exactly fair to myself and others.

Perhaps I am hoodooed by some wrong attitude toward some experience in the recent past. I am not writing this to blame you for anything or insinuate or imply anything uncomfortable. I hate to write it at all except that, if I don't, I'll be writing with stinted freedom and so I write as I feel even though I am not satisfied with myself. I'll have to ask you to overlook the stuff in general though because I know I am not this way always. I am not scared about this because it does not have anything to do with our rational love and I know it will all blow away before long, and you are big enough to help me out. But I haven't said what's wrong — well I don't know, and I have just been writing a lot of conjectures that may seem momentous, but they are not supposed to be because I think there's merely been some subtled negligence or mistake on my part that has started me to thinking in the wrong direction. I know it isn't your love's fault because you have put into your recent few letters more than I had any conscientious readiness to appreciate — oh, shoot, what am I saying? If there is any thrust in this letter, I positively don't mean it. I'd rather talk to you so I wouldn't run so many risks. And I know I could forget all this stuff in a hurry if I could enjoy your more satisfactory nearness. Then if I felt in the least this way, I could see it and we could discuss it; and if you didn't, you could better help me. I wouldn't have to write so much without saying anything either. I am afraid this letter will hurt you or at least make you feel unsatisfied or something, but I feel better for having written just as I have been trying not to think. It's all vague, but in general affect it hinders my love from being as enthusiastic as I know it rightfully and permanently is.

What were those misunderstandings about that you would like to clear up if you'd have me just a little while?

When I said it's fundamentally un-Christian to get blue, I hurt you cruelly didn't I? Isn't that the calling that you mentioned? Well, the forgiveness that I wanted is for having said it in that way, and I am sure you've given that. . . .

On Friday P.M. I wrote home to mother and also to Roanoke to I.N.H. He wrote me a birthday letter and I answered that besides asking him a lot of sincere questions about preaching. I hope they will be able to get us better acquainted. Really he is a stranger to me and I hate to miss the possible good that may come from re-acquaintance even under the unfortunate circumstances as they are. When I was home two years ago, I shunned him and hesitated to talk to him; but now I am willing and glad to give him all credit possible. I am thinking more and more of going east next summer. . . .

While we were waiting we walked into the classroom which was dimly lighted from adjoining rooms. Helser had been in before and looked around and saw a lady sitting in a chair to his left in a dark corner. He started to speak but saw her bare feet and found out it was a dummyess that they used in class work. He told me about it, but said it was made of clay and had its hands stretched out and up. So thought I'd see an imposing statue. But here in this obscure corner sat this form in a ghostly shadow. I shuddered and went out, and went in and shuddered again, etc. Say, it really hurts to be scared. Doesn't it? Even when you know you're safe. . . .

Esther, this has been about a mean letter. I ought to forget all that and write you a letter full of love without chafing features, but I am trusting to your bigness to overlook this mess and give me credit for writing uncamouflaged. I feel better personally for having written it, but perhaps I ought to burn it. I am still trying to be your sincere knight errant worthy of lady's love and uplifting to mankind. I want you to help me fill my album sometime. I am such a awkward mannequin at such things. A girl at my table is named Tusing. Is that sing-sing? And I am all yours, dear heart, mistakes, discouragements, and successes. Here's hoping that the last will out-weight. With mingled and vague thoughts, but sincere devotion, I am your bad boy, William.

This isn't supposed to be pessimistic.

(There is a handwritten note on the envelope of this letter, Esther's handwriting of many years later; "It's somewhat comforting to know he had his up's and down's too.")

* * *

From Akron, O., July 6, 1919

I work from 6:30 to 3:00 a day. Next week I want to work at night and so until school. I hate to change every two weeks as is necessary on day shifts. And I'd hate to work anytime from 3:00 to 11:30 ditto. I don't know yet if I can get on the night shift.

I got up and ate breakfast and straightened out my room and read a little and then it was time to go to Hartville for the United Sunday School celebration of four Sunday Schools. Nearly 100 Akronites went and had a bigger representation than any other Sunday School. The morning program included two talks besides the readings, songs, choruses, and exercises. I sang in the Akron Chorus. The Hartville mixed quartet rendered two songs. And I questioned seriously the advisability of having four folks stand up there and sing in individual keys. They did! . . . .

. . . . and then came home to find the house locked. Brubaker's gone and no key on me! High up on the porch wall was a box in which was a letter that seemed to bring new joys to my soul. It was yours in which you seemed so near I could almost feel you by my side in the porch swing like we were one night—you know when—and at a place—you know where. And I knew again that you love me. That is what rings in my soul these days. I am living therein. I'll try not to misunderstand anymore, and Esther, I am might glad for the spirit in which you explained to me. I feel much more bouyant now.

I trust you had a very pleasant 4th. I wonder how it would go for us to spend a 4th together. Wouldn't it seem strange? We have managed to pack Christmas full of significance however, and an Easter or two mean much. Then there is *our day*—Monday, 1:00 P.M., in the den, September 16, 1918. Ain't it great?

Yesterday Russell West came with me home from town. I was going to write to you then and work on my C.W. program for tonight. But West is such a good listener that I talked to him until 9 P.M. And I have ceased to regard that wasted which is spent in constructive visitation.

* * *

From Akron, O., July 17, 1919

No, I never read "Vanity Fair" but I expect to. If I remember, Thackery treats of and depicts one Becky Sharp in an environment around Brussels at the time of Waterloo. If that is right, mother told me the story once but that's all I remember. She told me about Oliver Twist, too, once. I just finished reading that this morning. I've been reading on the street car, but I couldn't wait toward the last so I read several hours here at home. I'll admit that it is a risky book to read in returning home at 12:30 A.M. when all is still in the house. . . .

For beauty, I am not a star,
There are others more handsome by far,
My face—I don't mind it,

For I am behind it;
It is those in front that I jar.

The one big comfort in plain features is that you don't have the sneaking suspicion and lurking fear that folks like you for your stunning eye or killing dimples or some such affectation.

* * *

From a letter dated July 21, 1919

I got Matthew 6:24-34 well in hand and preached without even a Bible. But the passage was familiar enough to bespeak its own context. And then I preached. Although I felt keenly the seriousness of the occasion, I determined not to be anxious while preaching a sermon against worry. I felt freedom and said several good things on the spur of the hour. But my freedom consisted in thorough preparation. I knew when and what I wanted to say. However, I did forget one or two fitting statements.

After service the folks seemed to be laboring under the assumption that I was supposed to be congratulated. There were several real ones out of the whole group, however, that bespoke a confidence in well-wishing that inspires one in an impelling way. Some congratulated me on delivery, some on effort, some on improvement, some in general, and some "just anyhow." I told some I trusted that I could, in the near future, congratulate them in the living of it. And furthermore, it was God's truth, not mine.

* * *

From a letter dated 7th of August, 1919

Well, say, when do we find ourselves in Chicago? Shall it be a year after the significant one? They are having Love Feast here on 7th of September for the special benefit of the college boys. Were it not for that and the difficulty of getting my paraphernalia to M.C., I'd like to come that Sunday. But I can bring you a self more settled in the year's work if I go via M.C. I don't like for this visit to be so short since it may have to last nine months or a year. But we can get right to business more than last year and I may get in there Friday night. Then, too, I think I can afford to miss a day in school a little better than a day here in the shop. But with all, when do you prefer? There are going to be two in this affair. and I desire not to be aribitrary.

* * *

On a letter dated Sept. 4, in which the postmark is not legible, the return address in the upper left hand corner of the envelope says simply, "Me—Here."

* * *

From a letter dated Nov. 28, 1919

My dearest girl on earth,

This is a very quiet morning; the dean, wife, and Bobbie are at Wakaroosa at the dean's home. They will be there until Sunday P.M. Paul Stoner is sleeping away his day, Miss Bose hasn't stirred around yet very much. Wilma Bollinger came over last evening with her bow and used the parlor here. It would go to waste otherwise. Frank Younger took Miss Bose to the basketball game Wednesday evening. Ask Mrs. Hazel and Georgia wat they opine regarding that. But she did not use the parlor. Miss Bollinger stayed the balance of the night with Miss Bose, hence there are two ladies in this household. That chickens have had a good breakfast of bran, mush and warm water this morning; the fire is rather slow. The snow is falling in spiratic flakes or balls like uncooked tapioca (not minute tapioca, but those little drops like pieces of cassava root.) The sky is overcast with a clammy looking steel-grey film, hiding the sun and wrapping the day in a subdued and somber gloom. The snow lieth about in blotches, giving the earth a modeled effect like a camouflaged battleship. The leaves or the trees are hanging in a crest-fallen and shivery fashion. They are of a sickly brown, all curled up, and very sparsely scattered over the trees. A few children of some neighboring clan are out upon the white and icy avenue piping and calling to one another. Now they are quiet, but Stoner snores on and the watches grind the seconds with a monotonous, yet fateful precision.

This table is bestrewn with letters, blotters, magazines, knoves, ink bottles, pencils, a whisk broom, a very useful handkerchief, and books! (The fire must be fixed now.) The girls are now up and around. Paul is beginning to squirm lazily about in as much as he has had two pillows piled upon his head by the winter. The fire is beginning to bubble up through the pipes and melt the chill of this room. The day seems brighter. The watches tick more snappily, and with a tinge of joy in their task. A woodpecker is rapping gently on the southeast corner of the house. Stoner snores again. The girl on the December is smiling through her eyes the love you certainly have in yours. And dearest Esther, you are longed for right mightily. Yet 22 days and this aforesaid longing will be shortened right mightily.

* * *

From a letter of Dec. 4, 1919

I am taking Shakespeare, 18th Century English, Public Speaking, and Roman History, and no girl. But I have one awaiting my coming and I'll be there if the trains run.

* * *

Manchester College, Dec. 7, 1919

My Dear Esther,

It is now Sunday evening. Night is wrapping her sable draperies about us and the day is hushed to sleep. Despite the rawness of the air, tranquility reigns supreme in my little room. This has been a very busy day and now that it's nearly gone, a longing creeps over me to fly to you, dear heart, for fellowship and love . . . not long, my sweetheart, my faithful love, not long will you have to wait in vain. For indeed, but little more than two weeks yet shall find me in your reach. Then I'll stand on my head, jump over a stick, turn somersaults, or whatnot even as you desire. Till then, I'll love you heartily as every day I do . . .

Fan the embers into full blaze against my coming and this shall be another real Christmas. Very sincerely,

William

* * *

Letter postmarked Dec. 12, 1919

Tuesday evening the lights went out and stayed there until next day. Last night they did too, but came on at 9 o'clock. However we had our lecture by presto-light. It was very interesting to me, but quite a few went to sleep over in the Mediterranean.

* * *

* * *

Letter dated Dec. 14, 1919

Well, I've been to a wedding of Trude and Floyd. We left here at nearly 5:00 and got back after 10:00. The roads were rough and the Ford back had 16 folks where 11 could comfortable sit. Miss Lantzenhiser was right in the middle on the floor. When we got out there, we had to couple off and march in . . . O, yes, and necktied preachers were scarce in our bunch. Roger Wenger had one on, but his coat was longer than Otho Wenger's. The ceremony went off very splendidly and I refrained from kissing the bride, also the groom. Miss Stutzman and Mrs. Schwalm sang two duets—"O Promise Me," and "Pray for Me." I really believe everybody ought to get married now. It certainly was convincing. If you would have been there by my side, I suppose we'd just have volunteered for a double ceremony. Yes, do you see us? . . .

Dearest Esther, I'm no boa constrictor, but I mean to let you know I love you. We'll see. Give my best regard to all your folks and accept a new cargo of love from your own lover.

William

* * *

Letter dated Dec. 18, 1919

Brush the cobwebs from your den or davenport or rocker and we will draw compound usery from them next week.
To you I'm coming, Love,
I'm coming soon to you.
Prepare against my coming, Love,
And joy will be our due.
Very sincerely, and even fondly,

Your own, William

* * *

Letter dated Dec. 31, 1919

My Dear Girl,

I am here as you may readily conclude. My registration card was 2319 instead of 3319, as it should be. Therefore I have run up and down this avenue in eager cold to find that house 2319 is right in the middle of the river. But I am now settled with Moomaw far enough from town to get fresh air. Delegates are coming in strong and hopes are running high.

Heltzer and I talked until midnight, and I got cold toward morning, but stayed right with my feet. My first night in a birth since I was little! I also kept that to myself.

Dearest girl, I am happy not only because you gave me more minutes last week than theretofore, but also because you gave me more per minute. And the blessed thing about it all is that it wears well and naturally after I leave. You are my girl and we'll have heaven on earth not long hence as far as farewell is concerned.

I have high hopes and sincere prayers for your love and happiness. Will you give Pauline what medicinal regard she is anxious to accept. And, sweetheart, my heart's deepest love is for you. Sincerely,

William

* * *

From a letter of Jan. 19, 1920

Then I talked to Bowers until midnight. We talked of childhood's escapades. I didn't tell him, but it is singular that my happiest days have been since February 7, 1916. Do you remember? I feel more like I have been an individual since then and to know that I possess your own generous heart of affection does indeed make one feel important. Bless your soul.

* * *

From a letter dated Jan. 1920

My own Esther,

Your love has colored every day for me and I am truly a happy man these days. God seems more real, Christ nearer, and you dearer than before. Really, Esther, I have just been saying to myself all the while, "That's the happiest evening I have ever spent." All the way home and ever since I remember above all your enthusiastic and natural love. I just couldn't help loving you more than ever before. I am so very glad you can love so happily even after you know me. And

I feel more confident of the future because I know you will stand right by me.

If your love is so encouraging and inspiring and wholesome now, what must it be when it shall grow without restraint! You'll find me ready for such joy, I am glad to be your sweetheart and have you for my own.

Very sincerely,

William

* * *

From letter of April 22, 1920

Esther, what do you think of my selling books? Are you telling me in the letter you are now sending me? Shall I knock on people's door and charge my commission for selling to them, or shall I produce tires and earn my money by boney-handed toil? Will you advise me? I'll be your liege man.

* * *

Letter from Mary Beahm, William's mother, to William and Esther, dated Dec. 9, 1921

(The letter was written on the back of an announcement of revival meetings at Hebron Seminary, Oct. 16—30, 1921.)

Dear son and daughter-to-be,

Please excuse the paper. There was no other convenient. The comfort is done—just finished and packed and Mary is addressing the package. Am hoping it will get out in the evening mail.

It is only a comfort. Not perfect. Any poor work you may find, please attribute to weakness of the flesh rather than indifference or carelessness in workmanship. The girls can help identify the samples. You'll find one of a suit "Willy" had twenty or more years ago. This is not a sample of dainty, fine, fancy work and ordinarily cover is cover when needed. What put me in the notion of piecing a comforter for each of the children was this quote, "While lying in bed so much unable even to read, I found so much pleasure in looking at the different materials in a comfort presented to me by Ridgely Aid

Society." Then I thought the children might find the same pleasure if ever so unfortunate as to be laid up. (Hope it won't be more than a day or so.)

Bruce Barton, in "The Legend of a Perfect Gift" says, "Money has no character. The dollar is equally at home in the pocket of the villian or the saint. You cannot express with money the intimate something that is you." Perhaps I can with stitches. Every stitch in the comfort was taken by my hand. Will you keep the house? Where? How I'd like to be on my way to Chicago in two weeks or less. However, it would be a big risk for me to take a trip like that in winter. May the Lord bless you both and may your happiness and usefulness be unlimited. Much love from,

Mother.

* * *

From a letter dated Jan. 31, 1924 to his mother

Dearest Mother,

I am sitting in my room with open window and I am dressed like an underwear advertisement. How is that for the last day of January. I am celebrating my rest day by staying in my room while my suit and overcoat get cleaned and pressed, and many of my clothes get washed. It's great to be lazy just for a day. And such a spring-fever day at that . . .

While my tonsils-itised, I recovered from a boil on my left jaw. I had one boil in South Dakota next to my left eye and another one in Texas on my left jaw. Hows that for a face! I got a cold sore on my nose, and it is just now about healed. So when I leave Wako, I'll have my shoes shined, my suit and overcoat cleaned and pressed, my clothes laundered, my boil boiled down, my nose healed and wiped, my hair cut, my teeth brushed, my face shaved, all clothed and in my right mind. I hope to go some distance before needing repairs again. . . .

Here's a question all missionary candidates must answer or stay off the field, to wit: What is it you sleep on at night, wash your teeth with in the morning, and sit on at noon? the answer is a bed, toothbrush, and a chair!

* * *

Hand Written Speech — Jan. 1920

The Origin and Significance of Arbor Day

There is an illusory idea among many folk that, by making play out of work, more will be accomplished with less effort. However true this may be in many of the communities wherein it obtains, I yet opine that, as Mr. Edison, Jr., said of his savant father, if one addressed himself assiduously to the task of learning to enjoy real work for himself eight or ten hours, he would get his work done more efficiently, than if he played, even enthusiastically, for sixteen or twenty hours.

Yet we all have predilections to be deluded into getting things done. When Tom Sawyer got his fence whitewashed by wheedling his human interest; a chord not at all cacophanous to any wholesome personality. Very little of our enthusiasm and animus is at all indigenous. On this premise are organized Ladies Aid Societies, "Swat-the Fly" campaigns, "Clean Campus" weeks, and sundry other movements for public benefit.

Fifteen centuries agone the municipal officials of the Swiss thorpe clept Brugg doled out one wheaten roll to each citizen who planted an oak tree on the village commons. Thus was the spirit of play put into the foresting of a Swiss cantor. This forest flourished and gave an added dignity and freshness to the town's appearance. Subsequently, each year the original planting day was memorialized.

This isolated incident seems to have been a precursor or prototype of the greater and more extensive growth of Arbor Day interest in America. In 1872 one J. Sterling Norton initiated the idea to the governor of Nebraska who in turn set aside a day for planting trees. On that first day, in their naive yet patent enthusiasm, the citizens of that western state planted a million trees which dotted, here and there, those receding and monotonous plains with new vigor and life. In 1885, Norton's own birthday was officially designated as the state Arbor Day while the day observed prior to that was duly abrogated. The movement won favor anon and has spread over our nation from the Gulf of California to the St. Lawrence and from Puget Sound to the Everglades. Enthusiasm grew apace and today Arbor Day is an appreciable and pronounced integral in our national life.

But why all this? What meaneth this indelible and deepening impression on our public life? Why all these haughty oaks, poplars, and maples with puissant arms stretched out to heaven and all these roots and rootlets delving thru the bowels of the earth with persistent ramifications? Because Arbor Day has grown around a highly generative idea pregnant with significance—the tree. Ergo, has it pushed its way to every obscure hamlet of our land. But what truth is embodied in a tree?

Beauty. From an aesthetic view point the trees have had a very far reaching effect in many of our towns. With a lengthening row of sylvan symmetry and verdure the inhabitants of the town felt all shiftlessness and insanitation repudiated. They were inspired to eschew all laxness of decorum and appearance. Muddy roads and ill kempt streets stood in glaring contrast beneath the shade of nature's own perfection. The gospel of decency and order, of beauty and symmetry, of cleanliness and nobleness was heralded from every leafladen bough. Children learned tidiness and acquired a keen taste for beauty.

Economy. The Arbor Day influence has been extended to the reforesting of many barren acres. From these are received wood, shade, and conserved rain-fall. Treeless plains are made to produce houses, boats, fuel, and beauty. Rivers have peered over the former high water marks and wells have been filled. Thus have famines been averted and man has been enabled to build a habitation wherein he could dwell.

Foresight. The most profound significance of Arbor Day is that "it is the only occasion devoted to the future rather than the past." It's returns are not immediate and are less selfish, Lowell testifies thus: "I think no man does anything more visibly useful to posterity than he who plants a tree." This I regard as the most happy significance of Arbor Day. It begets hope and faith in the future. It fosters a desire and willingness to invest their life now to gladden and serve unborn generations. It broadens sympathy and discloses new vistas of beauty and faith in days to come.

Thus has Arbor Day been permeating the life of our nation with new vitality and has won its place in public regard by its own merits and value.

CHAPTER THREE

"John and Figures —

Church and Chores . . ."

William and Esther served as missionaries in Nigeria from 1923-1937. The material in part one of this chapter is from a journal begun upon the start of their second term of service and dating from August 1924 to July 1937. The journal was actually a series of typewritten letters sent to family. William's descriptions and comments are typical of his style.

The Beahms spent most of their time at the mission station in Garkida. William taught, evangelized, and administered. He is still remembered in Nigeria. Natives say that he could race a bike over an obstruction or a ditch. And he spoke good Bura. In Nigeria, if you can fool or mislead another person, it is not a putdown, but a joke to be enjoyed by all. When a person arrives at a compound door at night, the practice is to call out a greeting. William was so good at speaking Bura that he would call out and people inside would think it was a Nigerian rather than a white. It was a source of merriment and joy among the natives. They would say, "Malam Beahm speaks our language so well that he can fool us."

His language facility, and his excellent memory of the ancient proverbs and witticisms of the culture enabled him to enter into the humor of the people. They say William would be riding along on horseback and see an old woman in a field bent over hoeing her peanut patch, and he would call out some sage observation or wisecrack too idiomatic for his fellow missionaries to understand; but the old woman would shriek with glee.

His skill in the Bura language enabled him to make a significant and lasting contribution to the church in Africa. The journal contains references to his work in translating the gospel of John. Before William left the mission field in 1937, he assisted in completing the Bura New Testament, translating the gospels, the Epistles, and Revelation.

The excerpts from the letters are typical of his attention to detail, persons, and descriptions. Idealistic visions of what missionary life is like may receive a slight jolt. The joys of teaching, evangelizing, and meshing Western and African faith experiences are here. But so is the tedium and perspiration of everyday things, such as weaving roof mats, supervising building, and keeping books as a treasurer. These were days of "John and figures—Church and chores."

The letters start on the boat as William and Esther leave for Africa, and continue until just prior to the birth of their daughter Harriet in September of 1930. It is a real disappointment that the journal stops before Harriet's birth, for certainly William's observations on his and Esther's experiences as beginning parents would have been choice.

Family was important to William. His immediate family was very special. He referred to Harriet as his "one little ewe lamb." Part two of this chapter includes one letter from Esther to her mother before Harriet's birth, and several letters from William to family after her birth and before the Beahms returned to the states. There are several letters from William to Esther after the family returned to the states, when trips away from home separated him from those who were most dear.

PART I

My Dear Folks,

13 August, 1928 Monday
The day has at last come around for us to start out on our second term of African service. One waivers between two diverse impulses. One is to dwell on the significance of this moment, trying to sum up

the joys and sorrows of the year of furlough, to gather all that has happened since four years ago,and to forecast all that may or, more likely, may not happen during the next three years. The other impulse is to be nonchalant and debonaire about it all and march onto the train with an off-hand "see you in three years." Well I believe we abade both impulses. . . .

14 August, Tuesday

We got into Montreal at 7:30 this morning. Looked around for information and found French signs all over the depot. After futile inquiry, we took a taxi and asked to be taken to the C.P.R. Hotel. He started out for a mile or so and then asked us the name of the hotel. We looked it up and found it to be Place Viger and said to take us to the Place Vaijer. He looked at it and said, "Oh, the Plazz Veezhey!" And we went to it. . . . At night we could see a blazing cross on the hill above the city. It was electric and not kukluktik. And so to bed.

15 August, Wednesday

The folder said breakfast would be served on board. So we ate only a bit of fruit last evening and no breakfast. We got on board, found our cabin, deposited our valuables, cleaned up, and then asked for our mail. Nice farewell greetings from relatives and friends. Anna Dunbar wrote a letter saying she was sending a parcel. It failed to show up. So within the final hour I dashed uptown through the hot sun to the post office and inquired in vain. Then I brought an armful of current magazines and dashed back to the ship all a sweat. No breakfast in sight. We sailed at 10:00 E.S.T. At 11:30 they invited us down to the dining room for seat assignment. No food around. Finally after we had been hanging limply over the rail, the bugle tooted and at 1:00 p.m. we found surcease of gnawing an accreditable menu. I broke the speed limit.

16 August, Thursday

We awakened in the wide gulf of St. Lawrence this morning. To the left of us on the north in Quebec shore. On our right to the south is the shore of Anticosti Island. This island has been the property of the great chocolate king, Menier. He has kept it as a wild game preserve, and it has been very famous as such. Now they say that it has been turned over to a syndicate to cut off the timber for woodpulp. So vanish the last securities of wild life. . . . We fell to talking with Mr. Smellie, the purser from Scotland; Mr. Verlinden, the steward from Belgium; and Mr. Follen, the librarian from London. Follen has averaged the distance three times around the world each year for 39 years. In that time he has spent two years with his family. On such separation of families is English shipping builded. The sea may unite nations, but it divides homes. Mr. Verlinden has a daughter who married a Mr. Verellen, who is an administrative officer in Mato, Katanga, Belgium Congo. He told us much of their life out there. The Brights and the Steinbecks leave Vancouver today for China.

17 August, Friday

We are going through the Straits of Belle Isle today out into the open sea. Before our lunch was finished we learned that an iceberg is outside. We dashed up and out to see it with our Kodak. We were too late for a picture but we could see it for a long time with our eye. It seemed to be snow covered or frosted and was beautiful both in design and in finish. We saw several smaller ones later in the afternoon. The air is cool as well. As we passed out into the sea one could feel the swell at once, although it was not great. Many were ill disposed at once.

18 August, Friday

Aye, and it is a bit rough today and quite chilly. Palm Beach clothes are out of style. We dress as for winter and wrap up in blankets for comfort. The sea is rough. Esther felt ill and remained in bed all morning. I felt twisty in my stomach, too. Too rough to ride in the cabin so I spent the day playing shuffleboard and reading Adam Bede. . . . I learned that there are several rum runners on board. They tell much of their experiences dodging back and forth across the twelve-mile limit. They look hardboiled but affluent.

20 August, Monday

This has simply been another day of rising, bathing, going to meals, playing shuffleboard, reading, walking, eating, walking, visiting, and so to bed. The only thing to break the monotony was a few reels of movie show presenting the making of paper. And a bit of Felix the Cat to top it off with.

21 August, Tuesday

The best number in the evening entertainment in my judgment was a series of water scenes given in pianologue form. The first part was real life. The man sang of a boy who leaned too far out over the canal bridge and fell in the water only to be scolded by his mother for having gotten his new trousers wet. The second scene was from fiction. A young lady fell into the water and was left struggling in last week's issue of our paper. A gallant young man plunges in to rescue her and they live happily ever after. The third scene was from opera. Plenty of music. Too much music, in fact. And lest we fail to understand the first time, the singer repeats again and again. The heroine falls into the water. The gallant young husband stands on the bank singing at great length and with great repetition, "Fear not, I will save thee," ditto, ditto, ditto. . . . " Then the chorus chimed in, "Yes, he will save thee, ditto, from the sea." Then the drowning girl gets a word in, "Ah, he will save me. . . . " The whole process is repeated several times until the girl is just rescued to death. The man who rendered it did so well that we laughed until our sides hurt. And so to bed.

22 August, Wednesday

Today we went over the ship, looking at the engines, the rudder, the kitchens, the third class section, etc. Twin screws revolve once a second. The coal stockers have a miserable, nasty job even though they do work only four hours at a time. Four hours on, and four hours off. This afternoon we busied ourselves packing our trunks. The ship is kind enough to take our trunks on to Antwerp for us so we can go via London without heavy baggage. . . . We sailed along south England all afternoon and saw its lights this evening.

23 August, Thursday

We eased into port, saw the Maurentania, passed the immigration officials, landed, went through customs, and boarded the train for London. It was nice and sunny so we got a delightful view of England. . . . We went on to Allisons and arranged our business, after which we went out shopping. We spent more time dogdling around and estimating the precise spot to board the buses than we did in buying goods. We wound up in utter disgust and went on out to the foreign mission's club on a steam train which filled the car with smoke. Dinner, evening, to bed.

24 August, Friday

We decided to go to Antwerp tonight and if we can get our things arranged, we hope to go on to Paris over Sunday. So we busied ourselves winding up our buying — sewing machines, helmets, tropical clothes, blankets, etc., etc., etc. Then we packed, drew our money, bought our tickets, and set out for Liverpool Street Station for Harwich and Antwerp. We finally pulled out and ran rickety split at more than 60 miles per hour to the sea. Then we boarded the Bruges and had a peaceful night across the channel.

26 August, Sunday

Today we joined a party of three others and were taken on a motor trip 60 miles away into Holland. We went to Merryburg and on to Flushing. On our way we crossed the national border where Queen Wilhelmina shakes her Dutch finger at King Albert. Then on through miles and miles of rich and clean green farmland and small brick villages. We saw dykes, canals, Dutch signs giving the "maximum snellheid." We saw windmills. I took a picture of one which was built in 1704. . . . On our way home we saw more of the same and got back in time to meet Brethren Emmert N. Bonsack and go with him to evening services.

27 August, Monday

This morning I went with the Brethren to do their shopping. This afternoon we went with them to see the sites. We spent most of the p.m. in the Antwerp Cathedral of Notre Dame where we saw Ruben's "Ascent to the Cross" and his "Descent From the Cross." It was a wonderful experience.

28 August, Tuesday

This is the farewell day. The passenger capacity of the Elizabethville is full—about 300. And there must have been 5,000 or 6,000 folk down at the riverside to see us off. These continentals are certainly demonstrative. Tears, tears, galore. And kisses by the thousand. Even young men would kiss one another repeatedly—first on one cheek and then on the other. And there must be 20 or more Catholic priests on board also. They look odd with their long gowns and their downie beards . . . We came out into the channel into a stiff gale, but the ship rode well being heavily laden. Later on we saw Le Zoute, Ostend, and by the moonlight we saw the beautiful chalk cliffs of Dover on our right and the lights of Calaias on the left. Spent the night in the channel seeing many lights and passing many ships.

30 August, Thursday

By the time we write a bit and exercise a bit and attend one hour of French class and an hour of lecture on the Belgium Congo and get our dressing and eating done, a day has gone by. We are on the Bay of Bisque but the sea is smooth as glass. There is, however, a bit of swell which is affecting many passengers unfavorably. Several of the bearded, gowned, tonsured, celebate, wine-drinking, cigar smoking priests had mal-de-mer also. We have delightful weather. We have 60 protestant missionaries on board. Much love. Beahm.

31 August, 1928, Friday

Today we are sailing over the old Spanish Main. Some of the passengers say they saw the lights of Cape Finisterre last night. I failed to do so. The sea is still calm and comfortable. Many ventured into their ice cream suits. The sun is good for basking. That is a pleasure we will leave behind for three years.

1 September, Saturday

Today we had two French classes. It is conversational French and it is hard as can be. We learn to read it and then we have to learn to pronounce it. Otherwise—cinq is sank! I ventured into a wash suit this a.m. and then it turned cooler . . . Mr. James L. Sibley is on board. He is the educational advisor to the Liberian government and has been interested in Negro education in the south for many years. He has just published a book on "Liberia: Old and New." I got hold of it today and fell to reading it.

2 September, Sunday

We passed Gibraltar yesterday, but saw it not. Now we will sail the balance of the way along the coast of Africa. In our protestant service today, Dr. Goddard of the Southern Methodist Board preached us a good sermon on "Honor All Men." The opening prayer and hymns and reading were all in French . . . it is much warmer. Many folk have spent the whole afternoon writing mail to be posted at the Canaries tomorrow.

3 September, Monday

We got up early for breakfast. After breakfast the coaling of the ship began on both sides and both ends of the hull from barges tied to her side. Most of the passengers went ashore in small launch. Our party of four took a Willis-Knight for a 16-mile drive way up the hillside. We went through the quaint Spanish town of Santa Cruez and on and on up to a town named Laguna. The island seems to be an arid one with irrigating reservoirs all over the terraced hills. Bananas, and other fruits, vegetables, and potatoes are raised in large quantities. We saw tropical gardens, cathedrals, donkeys, camels, Spanish maidens, coin divers, shawl and curio salesmen, etc. After buying some fruit in the market place and posting some letters, we came on back to the ship. . . . Islands are bigger in the sea than they appear in geography on the maps.

4 September, Tuesday

They have organized a series of daily sport events such as potatoe race, tug-a-war, cock fight, etc. This is to culminate next Tuesday when we cross the equator. I understand that "Old Father Neptune" comes on board to initiate all those who have not yet crossed the equator. It is rumored that all men will be thrown into a large tank of water, and that the ladies are sprayed with perfume after which Certificates of Crossing are given. I hope we all get through alive!

10 September, Monday

This evening about 5 o'clock we crossed the equator. Soon thereafter we heard that "Old Father Neptune" came on board. While we were at dinner, he came to the room blowing his horn. Then the names of all the uninitiated were read off. Tomorrow they will get their medicine.

11 September, Tuesday

It is still cool today. Remarkable weather for tropics. This morning the ladies each got a piece of ice down their back and some red marks on their faces, and some ice water on their heads, and some perfume on their dresses. The men got paste all over their faces, shaved with a wooden razer, and had a hose of salt water turned on them to wash it off. But they had a dress ball tonight. But before that, while we were eating dinner, each newly initiated person was presented with a certificate from King Neptune, proving that we had crossed the equator.

13 September, Thursday

We are now one month from Chicago. The boat stopped in the night. We sail up the Congo tomorrow. It is beautiful, wide, coffee colored. Much love to all. Beahm.

14 September, Friday

. . . At 4:30 we left on our small train. The track is about two and one-half feet wide. The train is to run all night and get us to Kinshasa tomorrow afternoon. Natives run the engine. Other natives operate the brakes on each car at signal whistles from the engineer. There are twelve of us in one car. Each has a swivel chair and each two chairs have a short shelf table between them. There are six chairs on each side of the center aisle. We are in this for the night. This arrangement would not be so bad if the car were new, clean, and cushioned. But the car is old, dirty, loose, creeky, slanting and crowded. There is no wash place.

15 September, Saturday

We finally got through the night. We got quite a bit of sleep, but very little rest and woke up filthy. Eating was a messy job, but we had plenty along.

19 September, Wednesday

Esther got wakened this morning by cramps and on calling the doctor discovered that it was not serious, that they found no ameba, and that she ought to be all right in several days. Later in the day we learned that several others were bothered, too, but not so bad as Esther. I spent much of the day caring for her, getting medicines, and hospital equipment, et al. By evening she had a temperature but fell asleep in due time.

20 September, Thursday

Esther had a fine sleep and feels a bit better this morning. She takes salts regularly which is worse than the disease. So the day passed by. . . . It rained this evening and cooled off the world.

21 September, Friday

Summer is now over and autumn is now here. But that means nothing in these parts. For we still wilt collars and soil cuffs and wrinkle drill (?) clothing throughout the day. Only evening and night bring delight.

Dear Folks, One and All,
30 September, Sunday

This morning we heard Kungo preach. He is a minister in one of the outline group of churches and is now here with a group of boys from his district who are hoping to enter school. He did a good job of getting response from his congregation. He even stopped long enough to ask the English visitors a question, get it interpreted, and get an Amen out of us. . . . This evening we went over to the single ladies house for a lap supper. After that, Dr. Lerrigo gave one of the finest and most interesting talks of a devotional nature that I have heard for many a long day. "Abide With Me." And he bristled with illustrations from biology and did it all in exceptionally choice English. . . . Home and to bed.

2 October, Tuesday

We had hoped to go north to the Congo River and visit the English Baptist Station at Wathen today. But a car will not be available until tomorrow. In the evening we took a long walk over to the native village and looked about and smelled the town over. We shall long remember it all.

4 October, Thursday

Today we rode third class down the line to Kimpese. The cars are open and dirty, hard seated and crowded. But it was a cloudy day so we did not mind the heat. . . . George Carpenter is here. I had a nice visit with him. He is an industrial worker and I enjoyed seeing his hydraulic ram, electric light plant, planning mill, etc.

5 October, Friday

We rode out to see the mission farm last evening. The Ford ran into a ditch and bent itself all up in front, but injured no one.

9 October, Tuesday

The boat is anchored off Port Gentil today. This is at Cape Lopez. Dr. Lerrigo says that Esther has malaria. So I spent much of the day watching and caring for her. She spent the day with aches and pains.

10 October, Wednesday

Esther is still quite ill, but her fever did not go up very high. It is too bad we have to get off tomorrow. Another day or so would surely get her into disembarking shape. . . . A party went over the ship this afternoon and I went with them most of the way. We went into all the refrigerating rooms. They were certainly very cold. The fish room was coldest. The fish are kept frozen all the time. Then they took us down into the motor room where we nearly burned up. Esther feels a bit better this evening, but is discouraged about having to get off being so weak.

12 October, Friday

Up early. Coffee at French mission. Then to the train in cars. About 9:00 or earlier we stopped at Edea, where the missionaries on the station had prepared a breakfast for us in the station. Good coffee, hot soup, and sandwiches! Yum, yum. I hope to meet those folks in heaven. . . . From Eseke we rode in a Ford sedan for about fifty miles with Dr. Good to the Bibia Station near Lolodorf. This is where Dr. Melvin Frasier of Elgin, Illinois, has worked for many years. . . . The houses are built entirely of wood—all but the roof. And the wood is all solid mahogany. They had a saw mill here to cut up the lumber. The walls and ceilings are all in paneled mahogany. A house like that cost $2,000. If it were at home in the U.S.A. and cut up into veneer, it would be worth $50,000. Mahogany houses and avocado pears every day in the year! Things aren't divided up right! But the main business of the place is to train preachers and they are doing a fine job of that on many young men.

16 October, Tuesday

Up early and breakfast. Then out to the "Ussukuma" in the surf-boat. Providence was kind. Not much surf. We got on board and got well settled. Sailed along until afternoon when we anchored in Victoria Harbor. This is the prettiest place we have seen. Now to Cameroon rising right out of the harbor, and her twin sister, Fernando Po Island, 70 miles away. We finished the day with the most gorgeous sunset ever devised.

18 October, Thursday

Rain and fog, but we reached Lagos before noon. We arranged to remain on the boat until tomorrow. Got our mail and enjoyed it heaps. All from the Eisenbises and none from the Beahms. They had a big dinner and dance on board this evening.

21 October, Sunday

I arose this morning at 6:30 and saw the Ussukuma glide majestically down to sea. We think well of her, especially for her choice German cooking. . . . We attended Christ Church of the Anglican Communion. We certainly had a gay time fumbling our uncertain way through their circuitous usage of the Book of Common Prayer. Up and down, down and up, singing, chanting, praying, announcing—always doing something we knew nothing about.

Dear Family—hither and yon,
23 October, Tuesday

Yesterday we traveled the well-watered area of the south. Got awake last night about 1:00 and found ourselves at Jebba on the Niger. By the noise the Africans made, this town ought to be called Jabber. For it sounded mighty like a large market in broad daylight.

25 October, Thursday

Esther Haw, we celebrated your birthday by sending off 21 boxes of groceries to Garkida on 19 men's heads. They cost $150.00 in New York, and cost $35 to get to Jos, including customs duty. It will cost between $90 and $100 to get them taken from here 280 miles out to Garkida, and the men will be on the road from 20 to 30 days. Who said time and space are subjective?

30 October, Tuesday
    Last year, Misses Sisler and Harper had their sewing machine stolen between Jos and Garkida. There are so many of them in this country that the packing box is well known. So we conceived the idea of putting the machine in another and larger box to insure safe arrival at Garkida. It is now in the hands of the Lord.

1 November, Thursday
    We got in touch with over a dozen Bura boys who are around here working in the tin fields or on the public roads. They range in age from say 13 to 18. Here they are alone, having likely run away from their parents. They walked all the way in and are living among strangers with a strange tongue. It is between twelve and twenty day's walk back to Garkida. But they forage absolutely for themselves. Get their own jobs, and live their own life. Imagine American kids at that age exercising so much self confidence and initiative. It gets very cold here, and although wages are twice as high, they save nothing, for food is high as well.

6 November, Tuesday
    We drove all night long, picking up catnaps as best we could. Clarence Heckman and Dr. Gibble took turn about running the Ford. The rest of us fell all over each other, tied ourselves in knots, ate tons of dust, shivered our timbers, and eked through the night in general. The Brethrens' grey beards were reddish brown today. Stopped at Damaturu to mail some mail and send a wire. This is our post office and we are still 115 miles from Garkida. . . . We finally pulled in at Buni, 70 miles from home and 220 miles from Jos. All were fully ausgespielt. We finally got nourishment, a near wash, and fell asleep.

7 November, Wednesday
    Breakfast, and off for the last time. Went through Bubiu mid-morning and started on the last 30 miles of impossible road. We bumped along to the Dzur River, 7 miles from Garkida. There we ate our last lunch while we waited for men to show up to pull our bus over the stream. Then up and down over the roughest possible roads to the Hawal—1 mile yet. It is less than 48 hours since we left Jos. The motor works infinitely better at night so we have made good time. Last fall it took us 6 days to make this same trip. We finally arrived at Garkida, and saw about 100 school boys lined up to greet us. Then

the school girls came tearing around. As we reached them, they all let up a great shout of welcome and we were properly overwhelmed.

8 November, Thursday

Our house and kitchen boys were waiting for us and were on hand today. We unpacked our stuff which had been stored away and began the gruesome task of setting up housekeeping once more. Today we ate with friends. We also looked around over the place a bit and noted the changes going on. Hospital building is nearing completion. Boys' school buildings are going right up. Roads have been improved. And best of all, the Buras are pressing into the kingdom and waiting to be taught for baptism. The Spirit has certainly been working this past year.

10 November, Saturday

I shot a big red monkey today and attended station meeting all morning besides. Dinner at Helser's tonight.

11 November, Sunday

Church in the Garkida Village this morning. All of the newcomers spoke and a number of the Buras. They are tremendously impressed with the grey beards and hair of the Brethren. They marveled that at their age they will venture out this far from home. And they don't believe that their mothers are still living.

12 November, Monday

It will be nearly two months yet before Annual Mission Meeting when it will be finally settled where and what we shall do. Until that time, we are to work in the boys' school here. So we began it today.

14 November, Wednesday

It is disappointing how many things there are around waiting to be done in order to get going again. Mats to make, to put up, rats to catch, meetings to attend, garden to look after, a thousand and one things to be bought, and it is no snap to buy things in this country. It takes more time off than the thing is actually worth. But we need it, and we do not want to spoil the sellers by paying too much, so the eternal oriental bargaining goes on a pace.

15 November, Thursday

Sailed along the day with business as usual.

17 November, Saturday

We got the boat mail which gladdened our hearts. Letters from our mothers were eagerly read. We also got a wire from Jos, saying that Herbert Hoover was elected by a substantial majority. They heard it in Jos over the radio, but it took the wire six days to come from our post office to us here. We trust that subsequent news confirms this information.

21 November, Wednesday

Our groceries are coming in, one by one, and we keep on wondering if it will all get here finally. It is a long drawn-out process. We could save bother, time, and money if we did not need to eat, but then think of the fun we would miss.

22 November, Thursday

The desert harmattan haze is hovering over us these days. It tempers the sun greatly and the nights get cool every once in a while. The bush land is dry and parched. Nearly every night we can see a bush fire somewhere or the other. The farmers are busy gathering in their beans, okra, pumpkins, and corn. Autumn's melancholy days are here.

28 November, 1928, Wednesday

It may get cooler later on, but I feel a bit disappointed in the coolness of the cool season. As I recall, it used to be cooler this time of the year when we first came to this country. I well remember one year we stood out on a morning hillside, seeing Mallotts off on a short motor trip and our skin stood thick with goosepimples on the 15th of November. Times do not seem to be what they used to be.

29 November, Thursday

There are a great many things one ought to do on a day like this. And were we in the U.S.A. instead of an English protectorate, we would likely do them. Esther felt so fagged out though that she even gave up making the pumpkin pie she had planned. Nonetheless, we are thankful for getting settled, for seeing the Bura children blossom out, for seeing the school children increase in wisdom and knowledge, for reasonable health, good food with fresh tomatoes daily from our river garden, for quinine, mosquito nets, boiled filtered water, mosquito boots, and all other helpful paraphernalia for good living here.

2 December, Sunday

This date was on Friday last year and your unworthy relatives steamed into New York, bent on furlough. That is what not quite happened to us — getting bent on furlough. Only by the goodness of our relatives and friends did we avoid being not merely bent, but broke. . . . I interpreted a sermon for Brother Bonsack this morning to the Bura Church assembled at Garkida. . . . This evening we all had a lap supper at Heckmans after which Brother Emmert gave a wonderful message on our high calling. He talks as one who has been on the mission field for other purposes than observation. After a day of weaving roofing mats, teaching school, and half-soleing shoes, we had a long church meeting tonight. It is interesting to see these young Christians take their church life so seriously. They delight in the mechanism of voting as a basis of selecting committee members. They try to be fair to both sides. The African predelection for debate and palaver ought to be an earnest for interesting council meetings in the future.

4 December, Tuesday

Prayer meeting over at Heckman's tonight turned into a free-for-all discussion of how to carry out a Dunker Love Feast in Bura Land. If we have only our American selves, it is not too difficult. Or again, if we simply had the job of guiding the Bura Church into having an indiginous form of it, that would not be beyond achievement. But the problem of having one with Americans and Africans together is a challenge to the widest knowledge of both American and Bura cultures and fine discriminations in trying to fuse them in a ceremony without making both groups self-conscious.

6 December, Thursday

We got a mysterious note yesterday, asking us to congregate in front of the mission store today at 3:30 with our own plates, tools, drinking water, cushions, and appetites. All of which we promptly did. After waiting for the entire group, we started off for the top of the hill to our traditional eating place. Large flat stones for a table, smaller ones (more or less flat) for others, plenty of fried chicken, potatoe salad, olives, bread and jam, scalloped corn, coffee, and fruit. Et all of it. This evening would have fitted in well for last Thursday. If I hear no objections, I will hereby make the impressions of today retroactive for Thanksgiving Day. What different does a week make between friends?

16 December, Sunday

Nearly the whole Love Feast preparation committee fell down on the job, and I had to go around all afternoon jacking them up. But seeing that all things were in readiness, we held the meeting this evening after a wedding and accepting a member into the church. We all sat around in a circle on palm slabs, American and African mixed up. The food consisted of stewed goat and ginnie corn mush. Each person furnished his own plate or gourd. Some ate with fingers while others used forks. The food was set in bowls on the ground before us. The feet washing was held outside, but there was no wall to the church so it was all in plain view of everyone. Everyone agreed that it was a very helpful occasion. We all enjoyed it a great deal. The whole Bura membership was there from all of the three stations.

19 December, Wednesday

We went through a long and strenuous day much like yesterday. Everything is secondary now but our discussions with the deputation and one another. And the year's grist of business is being sweated over from coal to morning through burning noon into cool evening.

20 December, Thursday

We are still going through the mill. Field committee met most of the day until we were on the ragged edge.

22 December, Saturday

Times have degenerated to the point where they have wished the job of mission treasurer on to me. I finally came to and went over to Gibbles today to receive instructions from Mrs. Gibble.

23 December, Sunday

This has been a full day. The mail came early this a.m., but I did not stay to read it. I hastened down the river to my village appointments and did not get back until 1 o'clock. We had just gotten to sleep for a nap when the church elders called and informed us that they wanted to ordain us to the eldership. So we got ourselves together and went over to the Garkida Church and were ordained in the Bura tongue.

26 December, Wednesday

There was no school this week. All were tired to death. So we spent a quiet peaceful day, letting our faces and nerves down. Love to all. William.

1 January, 1929, Tuesday

Clarence Heckman nearly raised the dead last night by shooting his gun, ringing the mission bell, and having a gang of school boys bang sticks on Standard Oil tins. We knew at once, however, what and who it was. But Dr. Robertson thought there was a house on fire and he came running over from the hospital hill in his pajamas offering to help. But by the time he got there the old year had died. Meanwhile his wife was sitting up in bed over there at their house wondering what in the world was going on and whether anyone needed her nursing care. But before the doctor got home to appraise her of the doings, the new year was born. Happy New Year to you all.

3 January, Thursday

After school this evening, I ventured out on a pig hunt. I saw no pigs. But ran head on to a large flock of guinea fowl. There must have been forty or fifty of them. I succeeded in shooting at them and scattering them into several groups. But to the best of my knowledge the most fastidious member of the S.P.C.A. could find no fault with any overt impression I made on any of them with my blunder bust.

4 January, Friday

Taught school again this morning. I had good intentions of doing likewise this afternoon. But the Haw Valley was on fire. And each year when the bush burns the whole Bura tribe turns out seeking for mice. The mice run into their holes while the grass burns over their heads. And immediately after the fire has burned, the Bura tribe advances with posied hoe and drawn bow to dig out buried ones and shoot running ones. Since I was fairly certain that about 79% of the boys would not be back in time for afternoon school, and whereas, I knew that this was one of the best chances of the year to get sufficient meat for a square Bura meal, and whereas I could not teach anything to anybody whose heart is out in the crackling bush fire, and whereas I have been a boy myself on several occasions, and whereas, etc., I dismissed school for the afternoon to take up again on the Monday morning next.

5 January, Saturday

I am still running a gang of women doing walls and wells. Also had to oversee half a hundred men putting on a grass roof. And in odd moments I oversaw the mission carpenter in making furniture.

19 January, Saturday

If fixing 986¾ things which have long awaited fixing constitutes a day's work, I did a day's work today. And so to bed.

20 January, Sunday

I rose this morning and was at my five-mile preaching appointment at 7:35 this morning. The mail came with letters from our mothers and our fathers and five different sisters. Christmas greetings are also filtering shame-facedly in. But we welcome them with open arms. If the writers remember them a month before Christmas, we ought to be happy to receive them a few weeks afterward. We are.

24 January, Thursday

Mail came today, including Emily Post. Esther has been buried in it every since. We are now learning how illmannered we have been. And we will know much better how to serve a proper tea to the next Englishman who happens along.

21 February, Thursday

We had the first district meeting of Africa today. Elder Kulp was moderator. Njida Gwari was writing clerk. Bukari Tarfa was reading clerk. It lasted all morning and a large part of the afternoon.

28 February, Thursday

Tomorrow is the beginning of the hot season. I'll be pouring over books out of every pore.

1 March, Friday

I spent much of the morning counting out the mission money, which is in my charge. It is a long, tedious and filthy job. And then it does not always come out right. We handle practically all of our money out here in shillings. Fancy building a $1500 house with quarters, dimes, nickels, and cents!

2 March, Saturday

While President was taking his last bath in the White House, I was winding up the heavy end of the month's bookkeeping. I hope Cal does not leave a ring around the tub for Herbert to wipe off with mutterings. That might be a good way to treat Al Smith, but I would hate to see him do Herbert Hoover that way.

3 March, Sunday

I dashed off to Garo this morning and preached the gospel under a tree. One old blind man continued to grumble about his ill usage by the Almighty, and wished he could die at once. I gave him a chocolate almond and called him uncle, and he smiled and came to church. That may not be the whole gospel, but it at least keeps him quiet long enough to teach his children who are promising.

5 March, Tuesday

Esther is doing the impossible stunt today of having tonsillitis without tonsils. She has a very sore throat. After teaching a bunch of restless little mites all morning, her talking had made it worse. I hope it does not last long. Mrs. Robertson bought some eggs which proported to be fresh. Later she went into her pantry and heard a cheap, cheap noise, and found in her closed egg can that one of the eggs had hatched out in one and one-half days, which is fourteen times as fast as it takes in the U.S.A. Of course, the Buras would consider her lucky for they regard nothing more delectable than an almost hatched egg. Well, why not!

7 March, Thursday

Esther is some better today although she stayed at home and rested. I am still sweating over accounts — personal and otherwise. My arms sweat and dissolve the ink. The books get all smeared up and I walk around here with somebodys private account all written over my forearm. This job is a mess.

8 March, Friday

South of us several hundred yards is a man named Mazo. He has been ill for several days. Although he lives about three hundred yards from the hospital, he has refused aid. He bought some medicine a few years ago for $ .50. It is to be used only in emergencies. If he uses it too soon, it will kill him. If he waits too long, he will not be able to get it out of his grain bin himself. And for someone else to get it out would destroy its charm. So yesterday or the day before, he struggled valiantly to get it out of his bin. Strong men carried his shaking form to the bin and helped him find it. He finally got it — a dab of grease in an antilopes horn. Some is to be rubbed on his neck and the balance he is to drink in hot water. The whole thing evidently failed, for he died today.

9 March, Saturday

I attended the burial this afternoon. While watching them lower Mazo into his cistern-shaped grave, one of the village head men said, "If you die here, we would be glad to give you a good burial like this. Oh, no, you would want to be buried in a box and be laid down stretched out so you could rott straight!" After the grave was closed, a friend took Mazo's bow and arrow and pranced around the grave awhile and then shot the arrow out into the unknown. It was a gripping symbolism of the man's departing spirit. Whither away?

10 March, 1929, Sunday
    This evening Esther and I climbed up the hill behind our house and looked down on the Bura dancing in honor of Mazo's death. It was quite warm and dry and dusty. These Buras who are accustomed to a little clothing, all pranced around there in thick groups, a milling mob eating one anothers dust and breathing one anothers unfresh air. It all looks like work to me.

14 March, Thursday
    What do you know about that! Last evening Mrs. Flohr—about 41 years old—was over to visit us. And this morning at 5 she had a 7½ pound baby girl—Annabelle Elizabeth Flohr. It is fat and has black hair. The night was cool and baby and both parents are doing well. All of our houses are one story bungalows. But that family lives in a house with five Flohrs.

15 March, Friday
    Ah, that girl just missed the Ides, didn't she? She is the fifth child to be born at Garkida, and the fourth girl. . . The Buras will soon begin to think that God means for polygamy among the young whites.

16 March, Saturday
    You could hardly raise any mission money by telling all the little odd things I did today. So to bed.

1 April, Monday
    Everything went on as usual today. Except, since it was All Fool's Day, custom gave one license to commit serious unveracities.

2 April, Tuesday
    We are back telling the truth today, and it goes hard at first, but we ought to be back in good trim by the end of the week.

12 April, Friday
    Bookkeeping will yet make me baldheaded. Abe Martin said, "When any man says 'It is not the money, but the principle of the thing,' why, it's the money." This may be true in general, but in bookkeeping, it would seem not to be true. For why else should one spend $10.00 worth of time looking for a $2.00 error?

21 April, Sunday

This morning we've looked down our back hill and saw the local chief, a father, mother, uncle, and neighbor drag a young girl bodily along down a stony path. It appears that she was determined to take her Christian covenant this morning. Her folks heard of it, and came over here very early and got hold of her. When she refused to go, they took her by hands and feet and tried to carry her. She squirmed so much that they could only drag her on the ground. Which they did. She was bare backed and had stone cuts all over her back. We remonstrated with them, but could not restrain them. It was awfully hard not to entertain less Christian feelings toward them than they manifested toward the courageous girl.

3 May, Friday

After an early lunch, we left for Garkida. We spent an hour killing 10% of a herd of ten grown antelopes this eve. But we still got home in good time for supper.

6 May, Monday

While I was not fighting my Bura way through the prologue of John's Gospel today, I was going batty over figures.

10 May, Friday

Here I am back at the hefty grind of John and figures, figures and John. It is just like chores and church, church and chores.

11 May, Saturday

When one goes to bed, all gooey and seepy with perspiration, it is easy enough to believe in ectoplasm. If there were just some way of lifting one's self up from the hot bed so a current of air could blow underneath!

28 May, Tuesday

This is the second day I worked to straighten out a 24¢ account. It surely must not be the money, but the principle of the thing.

1 July, Monday

Another full day on the books interrupted by a call to shoot a duck. I did and brought home twelve pounds of it—six feet wide!

3, 4, 5, 6, July, Wednesday to Saturday

What with John, river gardening, building some outhouses, and committee meetings, this time was shot four times in a row. Our two white birds of European size are doing well. The hen began setting on a half dozen eggs on the 4th. The rooster is a forlorn grass widower ever since. He has taken to eating peanuts out of my hand and follows me around.

8 July, Monday

Great tragedy on our hill: the grey hen which has been ten days on her eggs was found dead this morning. We hastily hunted another setting hen and transferred the eggs. It appears a scorpion bit her during the night. There was a big black spot on her back near her tail. And she was all curled up dying bravely at her post—poor bittie, she wanted eggs and got a scorpion!

17 July, Wednesday

We wound up the final chapter of John today. It remains to have it polished up and corrected and put into final shape for press.

18 July, Thursday

I have been going though Bura John with a local Bura to see if he could understand it. Sometimes I think it is passable Bura and then again I feel like it is a belabored piece of work. I hope it turns out helpfully.

19 August, Monday

We showed Mr. Dawson over the place today. We learned that he spends about $75 a month for whiskey and about $50 more for other strong drinks. One wonders that they accomplish anything at all. He must have thoroughly pickled innerds by now.

5 November, Tuesday

Stover Kulp is evidently so busy welcoming his young son, Phillip, that he has not gotten his monthly station treasurer's report in yet.

7 November, Thursday

This evening Mrs. Beahm and Mrs. Heckman surprised us by having a proper birthday dinner for us three men. There certainly must have been a missionary movement on foot about 1895, 6, 7. We had iced tea, ham, birthday cake, mashed potatoes, etc. After the meal, we played table tennis and the victrolia.

9, 10, 11 November

Busy with travel, field committee, and starting back. We saw the dear little Philip Masterton Kulp, and then we set out for home.

18 November, 1929, Monday
Today we went to the post office. How is that for news? Well it is 114 miles. We haven't been there for over a year.

19 November, Tuesday
After threatening to kill moon-baying dogs and night-braying asses, we managed to get a fair night's rest. One of the boys (Bura), who is along, has been marveling at the long clothesline they have up here. You see we have been traveling along the telegraph line all day.

22,23, November
The Preliminary Council of Missions met these days. It is much like Standing Committee. The rest of us sat around and got acquainted and raised more problems than we could settle.

24 November to 2 December
These days passed all too quickly in conference, convention, council, and committee meetings. We discussed relations with government, approach to pagans, Moslems, methods, aims, results, cooperation, unity, consecration, and service. We learned to know one another better and felt encouraged at the inherent spirit of unity of all our work.

3 January, Friday
One of our men married a Christian widow and it goes hard with the Bura not to have her turned over to a younger brother of the deceased even though she has stated that she did not want him. So we sat up on into the night trying to interpret native customs in a Christian way, conserving what is good and slice out carefully what must go.

11 January, Saturday
Many happy returns, Mother, You have been a good woman ever since I can remember and I gather from that you must have been a good girl before that. May God add many and happy and useful days. After the Bura manner, may you live as long as the crocodile, the palm root, the tamarind root and the mahogany stump. This evening the Emir of Yola drove into Garkida. He has four cars. And his salary is $12,500 per annum. Some chief.

2 February, 1930, Sunday

I celebrated Ground Hog Day by baptising my first man today. I had never done it before. The man had never seen it done before. So, be it whispered, we went down to the river this afternoon early and picked out the exact spot in the river and rehearsed as much as possible without spoiling the sacredness of the occasion. The man was so tall that the Buras remarked afterwards that after my hip pocket was under water, the man's knees were still out. It all went off tolerably well although I believe I forgot to ask him the third question.

5 to 9 May

We began moonlight meetings on Friday night. Just as we were ready to go, here hastened a lad to us. It was none other than the one who stole the cloth from Dr. Robertson's house several weeks ago. We thought he had skipped the country. But it appears that he walked 100 miles down to Yola and asked the jail keeper please to keep him in since he had stolen some goods. The jail man refused him entrance since he had no documents proving that he was a bone fide thief. So he waited around Yola several days hoping Kulp and Heckman would be returning from Numan and could give him needed papers. He got discouraged waiting for them over long, and finally decided to hot foot back to Garkida hoping to get the papers here! Then we went on to the moonlight meeting.

27 to 31 May

I had my vacation and did as little as possible. Now I must go back to work to get some rest.

10 June

Such a swarm of locust today! A rain headed them off so they slept just across the river — many Buras went out to get supplies of them for their next few meals.

11 June, Wednesday

The swarm rose this morning and lit out for our compound. It was ten miles long and three or four miles wide and, say, three hundred feet high, and thick as hops — just like a reddish snowstorm. They cleaned things up, believe me. It looks serious for this country this year. We chased them up and over the farms as best we could so they could go on and light on the next ones! The sun has darkened, the stars cease their shining, the moon has turned to blood. Just like Joel said.

4 July
   Hunted all day in vain. Found ice cream by nightfall.

8 to 13 July
   This is the happiest week since we came to Africa. West Bura, which has been closed to our mission work every since we are here, is at long last open and government is ready to consider our application for a site over there. Robertson, Heckman, and I spent this time over there talking to the residents and seeking a site. We finally located one thirteen miles south of Biu. It is on a year-round motor road. 1,000 feet higher than Garkida. In the heart of Buraland. And seven years of pentup hoping have finally been given vent. Future is before us and we feel the immediate and definite hand of God in recent workings. In stead of working among 2,000 Buras, we now have 80,000. Meanwhile, love to you one and all. William.

PART II

Letter from Garkida, Africa, dated March 1, 1930, from Esther to her mother

   This will likely be only a note. I only have one subject to talk about these days. And what a pleasant subject it is! You can guess easily the one all important subject with me — it's William, and next to him, it's his baby. We expect it in September. Of course, we are writing to no one except our two families. It is scarcely safe to tell it yet, even to our families, but it is so much fun to tell and oh so hard to keep.
   Naturally I am not feeling too well though I am not so bad as I had always anticipated. I feel and act as if I were riding in a canoe. A month ago I had my first examination and things were okay then. Today I should have had my second if the doctor were home. He has gone to Lassa to bring the Culps and Rupels over here to meet the governor. I wonder if others will be as surprised as we were. I had almost given up hope. About four days before I missed my first period, I sold a bolt of diaper cloth to Mrs. Culp. I had brought it out

when we first came 5½ years ago. I longingly told Mrs. Robertson that I had sold the cloth. She immediately answered, "Look out now, you will not get sick this month!" We laugh about it now, and I wouldn't mind if I had the diaper cloth to be hemming. . . .

This letter is all "I's." And you would be interested in watching our happy faces. We will be happier, too, if we can feel that no one is worrying about me. There are dangers ahead, but I face them gladly whatever the outcome might be. With much love, Esther.

* * *

From a letter dated May 10, 1931, from William to his mother.

Mother dear,

This is your day and you deserve it with all the rest. For you mustn't think you are worth only 1/365th of the year. We think of you daily, and love you always and try to serve as you would have us serve. . . . This eve, Mrs. Bittinger read us some beautiful "mother" poems. Then we gave testimonies of our mothers, and you are the best of them all. We prayed for you especially. God bless you.

Gardening season has come on. Harriet eats vegetables and chicken soup. She eats Cream of Wheat, drinks cows milk, tomato juice, cod liver oil, and quinine. She is a dear. She is like the Eisenbises early in the morning and changes into a Beahm during the day. Esther wonders what she used to do with her time. . . .

* * *

From Garkida, August 6th, 1931

Dear mother,

Just a note to say Harriet has 7½ teeth, weighs 18 lbs, will be 11 months old tomorrow, and is cute and dear beyond words. She crawls all about and babbles endlessly. We will be sailing from Nigeria in Jan. 1932, or the first part of February and hope to see you sometime in March. . . . . . . Glad for your letter and hope you have gotten stronger ere now. Strawberries, cherries, Anna's and Papa's meeting, et al sound good. Much Love,

William

***

From a July 17, 1937 letter to Esther, from Camp Harmony

Perry Huffaker and I comfort one another for he is separated from his wife and three boys until the first of September, as I am. There are some fine young folk here and they seem to have a freer and more wholesome outlook than when I was here before.

How I'd like to see you and whisper my love into your ear. I am doing it now. Do you hear it? And tell Harriet how I love you both. Best to the best.

William

* * *

From Camp Harmony, a letter dated July 18, 1937

Dearest,

22 years ago today I first met your clan in the person of Forrest. He was at the Bethany Building this p.m. with a straw hat which had green underneath the straw. How I missed you, I don't know. If I had life to live over again, I'd have met you that day instead of waiting until late September to find you at Manchester. But the real joy of my life is that I did find you at last, and I want to thank you again for the happiness you have brought and are bringing to me. . .

I do hope your convalescence is shoring up rapidly and that you will regain your strength without any depressing drawbacks—especially since I'll not be there to kiss you through them.

Be a good girlie, and we'll meet in a few more weeks. Ten days of our separation are over. And may God bless you and keep you. Love to Harriet, too. I love you heeps,

William

* * *

From Camp Haromony, July 23, 1937

My dear,

Two weeks now since I left you. It seems longer, but I am glad that much of our separation is over . . . . I certainly don't want you to suffer anymore. I think you have done enough for awhile. Tea enemas! That's a new way to get tead up. Which reminds me. I have had no coffee since here and a few leafy vegetables. But they give prunes and applesauce and raisins. . . .

Well, my fair ones, take good care of one another out there. Kiss and hug each other and remember that I pray often for you. For I love you very much and you are my dears.

William

CHAPTER FOUR

"Try Lepsog . . . "

1937 to 1962 were years of great contribution to the church for William. They were the days of teaching, beginning at Bethany Biblical Seminary in 1938 and serving as dean from 1944 to 1962 when he retired. He earned his Ph. D. degree from the University of Chicago in 1941. From 1942 – 1953 he was the secretary of the Annual Conference of the Church of the Brethren, and was affectionately known as the "Attorney General." Twice, in 1954 and 1959, he served as moderator of the Church of the Brethren, the highest office in the denomination. He served two terms as a member of the Church of the Brethren General Board, 1946 – 50 and 1957 – 62. While on the board, he served on the Foreign Mission Commission and also on the Christian Education Commission.

William's theology was solid – his exposition profound. But to use a favorite phrase of his, his teaching "bristled with illustrations" of all kinds – wisdom and wit sayings, word games, puns, and unique definitions. As an Elder in the local church, a member of the faculty, or a member of a denominational committee, he could work as hard and as serious as anyone. But you could never tell when the twinkle would break through. Sometimes his humor made a telling point; sometimes it was release; sometimes it was abrupt and surprising; but it seldom missed.

"Lepsog" is "gospel" spelled backwards, a fact you will discover later in the chapter. While the device makes a point in the story, it is clear he never hid his commitment to the gospel forwards. The church, *its ministry and mission, and God's people who make up the living body of Christ were central in his life. There are many such faithful saints, but it is nice to have one who carried his commitment liberally sprinkled with God's gift of smiles and laughter.*

This chapter is a collection of William's sayings and stories as well as vignettes shared by those who actually experienced or heard them in William's company. For convenience in reference, they are arranged in eight categories. The placement in a given category may be questionable to you. If the divisions get in your way, dismiss them, and at random, enjoy the wisdom and wit of William Beahm. All quotes appearing without explanatory notes are purely William's words.

1. MEMORY AND NAMES

William was riding a special train going through Williston, North Dakota on the way to Wenatchee, Washington. Ed Zook, then working for the railroad on a switch engine, boarded the train during its short stop and speaking to Brethren, met William. Fourteen years later, Ed met William for the second time. Without hesitation he reached out his hand to Ed and said, "Brother Ed of Minot, North Dakota; last seen at a short stop at Williston, North Dakota."

* * *

Required to preregister as a seminary student in order to get the 4-D draft classification, Jimmy Ross sent along a photo with the registration form. Over a year later, William was speaking at the Spiritual Life Institute at Bridgewater College. Between sessions, a friend suggested that Jimmy go over and introduce himself to Dr. Beahm. Having never met him before, Jimmy was surprised when William offered his hand in greeting and before Jimmy could say anything said, "Hello there, Jimmy Randall Ross."

* * *

At the opening of a seminary class, Jesse May Eller was surprised to hear her total name and more during roll call. William called out, "Jesse May Hinegardner Conner Eller." William had included her mother's name, her maiden name, and her married name!

* * *

In 1918 Walter Bowman's mother attended Manchester College as a student in the two-year normal course. One of her fellow students was William Beahm. After her Manchester experience, she returned to Northeastern Ohio, to the little town of Chippewa Lake, to school teaching and caring for a farm household. Although active in her local church at Black River, she had no further contact with the larger church until she attended the Des Moines Annual Conference in 1958. Standing in a family group, Walter introduced all to William, but when he got to his mother, William unhesitatingly said, "Oh, yes, you are Evelyn Krieger from Chippewa Lake."

* * *

William used to greet Chester Isaac Harley in two different ways. Sometimes he would say, "Well, I. C. Isaac Harley." Other times he would say, "Well, C. I. Harley?"

* * *

"William Alan Smith wrote a whole book called 'People Named Smith.' He said one of his friends had such a hard time finding a name not already used that he named his boy James Five-Eighths Smith, and he was able to hold up with his own identity with that name."

* * *

"Some names were related to the original owners. We know, of course, that those names do not necessarily have to carry those characteristics into the present. For example, we know persons whose names are Crouse, who not only do not have curly hair, they may not have any at all."

* * *

"I read of a man who said he moved from a larger town to a smaller town because in the larger town he was always trying to keep up with the Joneses, and in the smaller town, 'I'm, Jones.' "

* * *

"I remember speaking to Dr. Ira Morris Price at the University of Chicago, and asking him the meaning of his name. He said I wouldn't believe it, but the name was originally Rhys. That became the patronymic form Aprys and they snipped off the front, boiled out the middle, and came out where the Price is right."

* * *

Speaking of Harold Fasnacht, president emeritus of La Verne College, William said, "We have in our midst one named Fasnacht. I tried to find out what it means and it meant Shrove Tuesday. So we are privileged to have as one of the officers of our General Brotherhood Board, Brother Harold Mardi-Gras."

2. SEMINARY DAZE

"There is a standing rule that you are not supposed to learn anything in seminary until you pay the treasurer, but don't let that deter you from coming to class."

* * *

To a seminary class he said, "Before you celebrate your 50th wedding anniversary, examine this Bill of Particulars: 50 years of spring housecleaning, 600 months of rent and fuel payments, 2,608 weeks of laundryings and housecleanings, 18,262½ days of bedmaking, 54,787½ meals, menus, dishwashings and cookings."

* * *

Late one night, William suffered a kind of convulsion. When he came to in the hospital he said to Esther, "I'm going to school today." "Of course you're not." Esther responded. "I must," he said, "I gave them 'hell' yesterday, I've got to give them 'heaven' today." (It was a course in basic doctrines!)

* * *

Going about on campus while on a low-calorie diet he would sidle up to a colleague or student and whisper, "Got a ham sandwich on you?"

* * *

During World War II students at Bethany Seminary periodically had what was called a "foodless banquet." The meals consisted of a cookie or crackers and a glass of water. The regular price of the meal was contributed to Brethren Service. Generally on such occasions there was a speaker. On one occasion William had been invited to speak. There was a lack of understanding and when he failed to show, someone called him. He came immediately. He began his message this way "What I am about to share with you is something of a green apple. I am willing to go ahead if you are willing to suffer the consequences."

* * *

Charles Boyer sneezed abruptly and loudly in the midst of a class lecture. William paused long enough to say, "Geshundheit!" Chuck responded by thanking him in German. With that lead, William launched into a foreign language discourse that lasted about two minutes, none of which the students or Chuck understood. When he finished he looked at Chuck and said, "Now, you should be well blessed."

* * *

The classrooms in the old Bethany Seminary had very thin walls. William was teaching Christian ethics in one room and in the next room Floyd Mallott was teaching wisdom literature. On one occasion Mallott roared forth, "Why do the righteous suffer?" Hearing the words through the wall, William turned to the class, "I don't know, do you?"

* * *

An eye opener William Beahm style was this verse with which he greeted an early morning class: "In these days of indigestion it is really quite a question what to eat and what to leave alone; for each germ and each bacillus has a different way to kill us."

* * *

Paul Robinson, president of Bethany Theological Seminary, and Dean Beahm were working on weight and had a lunch consisting of pineapple juice mixed with Knox gelatin. The question was raised, "Shall we give God thanks for our food?" They decided it was more honest not to. As William noted, God was probably saying, "don't kid yourself or me."

* * *

President Robinson commuted from Chicago to Villa Park each day in a Volkswagon "bug." Beahm's comment about the relationship of Dr. Robinson's size and the car was, "I marvel everytime I see the president wrap himself in his V.W."

* * *

William made a very caustic remark in a faculty meeting. Almost-new faculty member Graydon Snyder added his feelings, which were even more disagreeable than William's. As if he had been waiting for the right time, William looked at Graydon and said, "That's a snider remark than I made."

* * *

When the bell had rung for class to begin, he paused a moment, quietly surveying the class, then greeted his early morning students, "Good morning, how are your drives today?"

3. THEOLOGY NOTES

"There are some who dwell entirely upon that of God in every man and overlook the deep twist of evil which erupts now and then in unexpected places. We see the analogy of understatement in the story of the elephant who looked down his trunk at the mouse and said, 'Why are you so small? Why aren't you as big as I am?' To this the mouse gave the squeeky reply, 'I been sick.' It is too light an appraisal to regard man's basic difficulty as ignorance or finiteness or immaturity, or even trauma."

* * *

"Grace and salvation are unnecessary apart from sin. I once knew a doctor who could only cure people with fits. If they didn't have fits he would give them fits and then cure them."

* * *

"Extending the Church through Christian Mission should not be limited to one or two acceptable methods. It should be a lavish uncalculating effort. Bet on every horse and put eggs in every basket."

* * *

"The words of the gospel are not sweetness and light, but salt and light."

* * *

He greeted his class in basic doctrines one morning by saying, "Brothers, today we are starting the subject of good and evil, and I tell you, there is more to it than meets the eye."

* * *

On the difference between privacy and secrecy, he said, "The fact that I have sexual relations with my wife is no secret, but it is, I tell you, darn private."

* * *

Being a particular man, he encouraged care and exactness in his students. After asking the class, "Why should we be so intent on a little vowel or a consonant?" he gave two examples: "A proprietor called the neon sign company with much anxiety. The B in his sign had gone out. The sign was supposed to read 'CAN'T BEAT OUR HAM-BURGERS.' There is also the husband who wrote his wife a card from Philadelphia saying, 'Am having a fine time — wish you were her.' "

* * *

"Christ's sacrifice was not because of a martyr complex. Jesus did not stick his neck out merely to get his throat cut."

* * *

In a lesson on the Kingdom of God, he said, "The kingdom may come by sudden and also by gradual processes. As C. D. Bonsack said, 'A clap of thunder and a flash of lightning are more thrilling than a drizzle, but the drizzle makes more clover.' "

* * *

"Revivalism tends to minimize the solid values of steady teaching and exemplary living. Revivals do to staunch church members what a glamor girl does to the ordinary faithful husband, or what the handsome swooner does to the girls when he makes the garden variety of boyfriend look insipid."

* * *

On the contagious quality of Christ he said, "He was a rash and not an eruption, if I may speak in measley terms."

* * *

The Brethren have no creed other than the New Testament. In a class discussion on the New Testament being sufficient for faith and practice, a student questioned, "Isn't the New Testament, however, a credal statement of the church and men?" "Behold," William replied, "a Philistine in our midst. I perceive some of you have been tampered with. Some of you have been blown upon by strange winds."

* * *

"The Bible is a grim book. It calls sin 'sin.' If need be, it would call a 'spade a spade' as we would say today."

* * *

"I think Jesus speaks as a Hebrew who throws terms at us. And if one doesn't catch the meaning, he'll give us another one; not to set grades of meaning within his phrases, but to throw at us a mosaic of living beauty and truth."

* * *

"Unless emotionalism is tied to something greater than itself, it is a mere fizz."

* * *

On adequate and inadequate concepts of sin, he said, "sin is more than specific acts we do or don't do. There are those who wouldn't swear or drink, but by their attitude they make others around them want to do both."

* * *

"It is not prayer that changes things, God does. It is something like a long belt on a threshing machine. The belt does not change things, the tractor does."

* * *

In a discussion on the relationship of theology and the social gospel, he said, "You must teach people arithmetic before they can understand the trinity."

* * *

On the matter of discerning the spirits, he said, "The true spirit isn't known by temperature readings. The slope of spiritual ecstasy is steep and slippery. There is a limit to ecstasy until it becomes dangerous."

* * *

On the relationship between forgiveness and repentance, he said, "We have bliss on the one hand and blisters on the other."

* * *

"We know what the man meant when he said, 'Repentance is like breaking a bone again to set it straight,' and we know the meaning of the phrase 'Jesus never hid his scars to win a disciple.' "

* * *

"The trinity is like a three-legged milking stool. The whole stool is God, and the legs are the Father, the Son, and the Holy Spirit."

* * *

He liked pithy things other people said. He quoted with relish this definition: "A philosopher of religion is a blind man in a dark cave at midnight trying to find a black cat that isn't there. A theologian, however, is a fellow who claims to have found the cat."

* * *

"Sin is like a raspberry seed under God's denture."

4. WISDOM AND WIT

"When I was a child, we moved every two years. In the church, three moves is equal to one being fired."

* * *

William looked long and hard at a salad served by a women's group at a district meeting. It consisted of green jello with chunks of cottage cheese and other red and purple goodies suspended through it.

He toyed at it with a fork and said, "For fear it may taste the way it looks, few will even start—if it does, none will finish."

* * *

He once said of a theologian, "That man can delve the deepest in the murky waters, stay down the longest, and come up the dryest of anyone I know."

* * *

"The most attractive quality of some gospel songs is they have pelvic persuasion."

* * *

"The only military experience the man ever had was to hear the *Charge of the Light Brigade* read with great feeling."

* * *

"Solomon was supposed to be so wise, but can you imagine day after day walking into the bathroom and getting tangled up in a thousand pair of nylons?"

* * *

"We have some freedom to choose, but there are many areas in which we are not free. We do not get to pick out parents, the country into which we are born, or our sex. In fact, the only thing I ever got to pick was my teeth."

* * *

"I learned as a boy, the only way to eat a grape is to squeeze out and discard the middle, peel what you have left, and eat the rest."

* * *

"An elder is an overseer and a supervisor according to the New Testament. What that means is that a good elder knows what to oversee and what to overlook."

* * *

Of an unfavorite writer he said, "He's like the Platt River—two feet deep and a mile wide at the mouth."

* * *

"The way to get into the cinema without paying is to go the exit door and get into the line of people coming out of the theatre—and back up slowly."

* * *

"I don't care how much you say, just so you say it in a few words."

* * *

When someone in a 1949 Annual Conference Planning Committee suggested a foodless banquet at the conference, he responded, "Oh, you mean an Old Mother Hubbard banquet."

* * *

"If you are nasty enough and keep it up long enough, you may get your way."

* * *

"Only when grafted from a producer did our orange seedling bear blossoms."

* * *

"One never falls in love with womankind."

* * *

"Sin is central, not peripheral, in the experience of man. You can't clean up the water by painting the town pump."

* * *

William was probably not the first nor the last to do it, but he did it. On Friday, the day for leftovers at Manchester College, he prayed, "Father, we thank you again for this food." The dining room was convulsed in laughter. That afternoon William was invited to visit the president.

* * *

"Fact is what we have to keep our faith from getting red."

* * *

"We lean upon the man we wrestle with."

* * *

The minister leading the opening of a district conference in Illinois and Wisconsin misread the text. When he came to "sexual immorality" he read it "sexual immortality." It was hardly out until William nudged me and said softly, "That's more than I hoped for."

* * *

"Tying apples on a lilac tree is not permanent."

* * *

One Sunday morning at First Church of the Brethren, Chicago, Pastor Harper Will quoted, "Abu Ben Adam." With dramatic flair, he concluded the poem, "Abu Ben Adam's name led all the rest." William leaned over and whispered to the person next to him, "Alphabetical order!"

* * *

"Intercourse in marriage is like the love feast and communion in the church. Both tend to mend and reaffirm the relationship."

* * *

"My grandpa used to say, 'When it rains too hard to cut wood in the woodshed, we go fishing.' "

* * *

"The wicked fleeith when no man pursuith, but he will run a heap faster if you get after him."

* * *

In the summer of 1952, he attended a wedding in Chicago. It was a beastly hot day. At the reception, he said to the bride and groom, "You weren't married, you were spot welded."

* * *

William returned to the Akron City Church of the Brethren, the church where he was ordained, for a special service. There were elaborate decorations of ferns and floral pieces around the pulpit. Being short of stature, as he stood to speak he couldn't see the congregation for the ferns. Leaning forward, he parted the greenery and began his sermon with, "The voice of one crying in the wilderness."

* * *

"Sin is like a Chinaman on a toboggan—Whee! easy go down, hard back up."

* * *

"If one is a scholar, he cannot be a fundamentalist; and if one is a fundamentalist, he cannot be a scholar."

* * *

"A delta is a river with its mouth full of mud."

* * *

"There are two famous noblemen in the Bible: Lord Howlong and Baron Figtree."

* * *

"The new hypocrisy is appearing worse than we are."

* * *

"To influence people, you must have some purpose other than winning friends."

* * *

Of a long time secretary at the General Offices of the Church of the Brethren, he said, "One of her great attributes is the ability to keep silent in seven languages."

5. WORD PLAY

"Dealing with the problem of keeping up with the Joneses by withdrawal is madness indeed. We are made for one another. Robinson Crusoe had hard going until Thursday evening; but come Friday, life began to pick up again."

* * *

Of a person who had been through extensive counseling, he said, "I think that man is suffering from paralysis of analysis."

* * *

Passing the city hall in Broadview, a Chicago suburb, several days after Marvin Dierks, a professor at Bethany Seminary, had paid a speeding fine, he commented, "There is the house that Dierks' jack built."

* * *

After a friend had given him a lift to a meeting and back, he got out of the car and said, "Thanks for taking me fro and to."

* * *

One Sunday morning found William in the hospital after being involved in an automobile accident. A visitor entered inquiring about his health, and he said, "Well, yeah, I'm all right except I have a hole in my head." Which he did! A big ugly gash. With only a slight pause, he continued, "I needed to be laid up here in the hospital like I needed a hole in the head."

* * *

It was not unusual to hear William answer roll call by saying, "A little Beahm in darkness, let it grow."

* * *

One time, at Elizabethtown College, William was seated at a table with Harold Bomberger and the girl Harold was later to marry, Betty Mann. Betty was a member of the Evangelical Congregational Church in Columbia, Pa., and her name was therefore not familar to William. After some time, he leaned over to Harold and asked, "Harold, is this Mann woman a Brethren sister?"

* * *

William enjoyed spoonerisms. When he didn't feel good he often spoke of feeling "meek in the widdle." One day in class he referred to Dr. Pangborne as Dr. Birthpangs.

* * *

William had special names for two women who worked at the Church of the Brethren Offices. Grace Hollinger was "Amazing Grace," and Hazel Peters was "Bewitching Hazel."

* * *

In 1958, there was a 250th Anniversary Celebration of the founding of the Church of the Brethren. In January, there were special events at Germantown, Pa., site of the first Brethren congregation in this country. It was announced at the meeting that the moderator, Desmond Bittinger, would be unable to be present because of illness and surgery. Later, when asked the nature of Brother Bittinger's surgery, William replied, "Whereas Brother Desmond once had a colon, now he has a semicolon."

* * *

When someone asked him why he came late to dinner at Manchester College, he said, "I've been reading about Pompei-i-i-i-i."

* * *

He was aware that a student's wife, Goldie Roller, had given birth to twins during the night. When he got to Bob's name in the roll call, he paused and said, "Boys, we are one of the few classes in theological education in this country with a student who has a roller bearing wife."

* * *

After an analysis of the particular quality of doubt exhibited by the disciple Thomas, he noted wryly, "Still, half of the cats in the world are named after Thomas."

* * *

He often used German words. At one point as he was taking apart a stubborn gadget, he mumbled that he could not find the "Unknupfungspunkt," which he translated to mean the unbuttoning point.

* * *

Observing a reckless driver on the highway, he said, "If he continues driving like that, most likely down the road a ways one of his friends will have to come along and scrape up an old acquaintance."

* * *

A student asked what necromancy was. He responded, "Said one person to another, 'I live in the house by the side of the road where the race of people go by.' Asked a second, 'Who won the race?' Said the first, 'I don't know, but they were neck and neck when they passed my place.' That's necromancy."

* * *

"When an Irishman was asked how he managed to bring in fourteen German prisoners, he replied, 'Faith, and I surrounded them.' "

* * *

When daughter Harriet and her husband Earl had their second child, he announced to the class, "Boys, I'm batching it for several days. My wife is in Pennsylvania having a grandson."

* * *

While we waited for a stop light in Chicago's Loop, a very shapely young lady crossed in front of the car. "One is tempted to watch with the naked eye," he said.

6. ANNUAL CONFERENCE

As moderator of Annual Conference at Ocean Grove, William led the delegates down through the agenda, A, B, C, D, E, and F. After caring for item F, he went on to item G. He announced it as, "Gee! Women in the ministry!" As item G was finished and they prepared to move on to the next item, William announced, "Now we can go to H!"

* * *

At the 1959 Annual Conference at Ocean Grove the weather was cold and rainy most of the week, until Saturday morning. Saturday was a bright, beautiful day. Beahm commented that, among other announcements, he wanted to extend "congratulations to Ocean Grove this morning for having a little sun." One brother (perhaps it was an Englishman) said he couldn't understand why everyone laughed when Brother Beahm reported that Ocean Grove had a little boy this morning.

* * *

At an Annual Meeting which he was moderating, many of the delegates who wanted to speak were standing too far from the microphones for the instruments to pick up their voices. After continual reminders to "stand close," he finally said to one of the speakers, "Brother, we could hear you better if you would take hold of the microphone and kiss it."

* * *

During the Colorado Springs Annual Conference, Dr. Calvert Ellis was moderator, and William was writing clerk. Rufus Bowman, a very large man, sat down on a chair; the chair broke and he went right on down to the floor. There was concern about him being hurt, but as he began to chuckle at his own predicament, William reached for the mike and said, "Brother Rufus Bowman has the floor."

* * *

To Annual Conference Standing Committee, charged with previewing all conference business, he said, "Our function is like a rabbit's front feet — that is, keep out of the way of the hind feet."

* * *

William was small of stature. While moderator of Annual Conference he stood up and found that the microphone needed to be raised in order for him to speak into it. While working to raise it, he commented, "It has taken me 55 years to discover that I am too tall."

* * *

One of the fraternal delegates to Annual Conference during a year that William was moderator had the last name Neher. When the delegate had finished his greeting, William said, "We've had a great experience together. We've been visiting and 'you-hooing' one another. There's a text for what we've been doing: 'You who were far off we now call Neher.' "

7. THE CHURCH

"It's interesting to note that Jesus took thirty years to prepare for a three year ministry. We take three years to prepare for thirty years of ministry."

* * *

"Too many ministers have a pathological meekness."

* * *

"Men, when you are in the parish, relax a little — don't take things too seriously. Lying awake nights trying to resolve all the problems of the parish makes you a pastoralcolic."

* * *

In reflecting on some of his experiences in Nigeria, he shared how difficult it was there to convert people from the Islamic faith to Christianity in view of the fact that polygamy was allowed in Islam, but not in Christianity. "There is a text," he said, "to describe our Christian missionary effort among the Mohammedans — 'We have fished all night and caught nothing.' "

* * *

"I don't know what would satisfy the average Dunker congregation in matters of a minister's wife — perhaps either bachelorhood or polygamy."

* * *

"When a church comes alive, it has problems. A dead church is easy to serve. The easiest part of the church to manage is the cemetery."

* * *

"Too many ministers are the putterers-in-chief of the congregation."

8. PERSONAL THINGS

"I have eighty cousins and one half dozen uncles and aunts with no children. Once a sister from Elizabethtown, Pa., asked my uncle Rufus Bucher how many children a Dunker preacher should have and he said, 'Sister, that's none of your business.' "

* * *

A favorite phrase upon returning home after an extended trip: "It's sure good to be back to your own vine and fig leaf."

* * *

After hearing a man give an address on "The Peril of Theology" he said, "Now I would like to give an address on 'The Peril of No Theology.' "

* * *

Physical characteristics were of interest to William Beahm. If he saw someone with a protruding chin, he would say, "That person is leading with his chin." Or at the same time if he saw someone with a large, protruding abdomen he would say, "That person is leading with his belly button."

* * *

When he was writing his book, "Studies in Christian Belief," the work went painfully slow. He told a friend, "I write a sentence, then contemplate it awhile. Then I put in a comma. Come the morrow, I'll take it out."

* * *

During the 1950's work was in process on the Eisenhower Expressway which passed alongside Bethany Seminary. Bricks from the torn down buildings were free for the taking. William later built a patio in the back of his home in Lombard with the confiscated bricks. He often laughed as he hauled them home in the trunk of his car how wonderful it was to steal bricks and not be arrested.

* * *

At a district mass rally, William was the featured speaker of the evening. The event was held at a district camp and several districts were represented. The meeting started about 7:30 and droned on with many different things taking place in the service before William was even introduced. At about 9:00 the worship leader introduced him and said, "We have given Brother Beahm the freedom to choose his own subject." William came to the speaker's stand and began by saying, "I would rather have been given the freedom to choose my own time."

* * *

In 1954 William was visiting Brethren Service Commission work in Austria and, with Don Durnbaugh, visited a family who had received a gift heifer. The family was very happy to see a B.S.C. representative and insisted that Don and William take refreshments with them. They served milk from the cow and homemade bread. William was much moved by the experience and commented on the way back to Linz that it was as true a communion experience as he had ever known.

* * *

During his term of service as a member of the General Brotherhood Board of the Church of the Brethren, William served on the Foreign Mission Commission. At one session, there was discussion of personnel. In a non-direct manner, the Nigerian Field had requested that a long term single missionary not be returned to the field — not because of anything she had done, but because there was some question about her effectiveness and the use of the church's money. The commission was about ready to accept the recommendations when William said, "When a person has served long and faithfully and is no longer effective as a younger person might be, there is no support in the scripture or in human decency to let them go. Tell Nigeria they'll have to use ingenuity or long suffering, and keep her in service." And they did.

* * *

A week or so after Mrs. Beahm had received a broken rib in an accident, he asked his class, "Have any of you fellows tried to love your wife when she has a broken rib?"

* * *

On behalf of the General Board of the Church of the Brethren, William toured the Nigerian Mission Field with Leland Brubaker, at that time Secretary of the Foreign Mission Commission, and Julian Gromer, an excellent photographer then living in Elgin, Illinois. The three were very congenial, so not every minute of their time was given to the important assignments which took them to Africa. Leland loved coffee, and though it was scarce in the late forties, he managed to find a supply of instant Nescafé and carry it with him — a veritable treasure in his suitcase. Often after a meal in a restaurant, or a home, Leland would whip out his hoarded coffee, get boiling water, and with great relish, savor the fruit of the tropics. In the course of their tour they arrived in Jos, where the school for missionary children was located. There William found two young boys very willing to be partners with him in a little scheme. Swearing (or affirming as the case may be) them to secrecy, he sent them to the workshop of Clarence Heckman with the instruction to bring back two cups of very fine sawdust, one of mahogany and one of ebony. By the time Ralph Royer and Philip Kulp had returned with the sawdust, William had lifted the jar of coffee from "Uncle Leland's" suitcase. He mixed the sawdust to look like coffee, emptied the real coffee into another container, and put the same amount of sawdust into the coffee jar. Then he placed the jar in its proper place in the suitcase. On the train, enroute from Jos to Lagos, Leland felt the pangs of coffee hunger, and ordering hot water, he poured it over a spoonful of his treasure. Instead of dissolving, it floated to the top! After listening to Leland fume for several hours about custom officials who had stolen his coffee, William finally gave him the real stuff.

A sister once said to William, "Why is the 'h' in your name?" He responded, "It stands for where I'm going when I die." She was horrified and said, "Brother Beahm!" He responded dryly, "Well, I plan on going to heaven, don't you?"

* * *

On the trip to the African Mission Field, Leland Brubaker and William were together at a meeting in which Leland had been asked to speak. They were about to give him a native interpreter, but William, who had mastered the language well during his term of service, asked if he might be allowed to try to interpret. The people were delighted for "Malam Beahm" to assist. Leland began his speech by saying, "There comes a time in the destiny of human affairs when the whole history of mankind is in the crucible of change." William translated with a very short sentence in Bura. Leland looked at William and said, "What did you say?" William replied, "I said, 'He greets you in the name of Jesus Christ.' Now from here on take it easy!"

* * *

A concerned sister approached William and asked him in hushed tones, "Is it true, Brother Beahm, that in Africa the natives don't wear any clothes?" "That's not true," he said, "except when we baptize them."

* * *

One time when William had been hospitalized following a late-night seizure, John Eller, administrator at Bethany Hospital, went up to the fourth floor to see him. When he walked in the door, William looked at him, smiled and said, "Fancy meeting me here."

9. STORIES AND SPEECHES

"A man, thinking to be helpful to a friend, pulled a string that was on his suit. He kept pulling and the string kept coming. When the man got home, his underwear was entirely gone."

* * *

"A brother, a bit shocked at what he saw on his first trip to Annual Conference, wrote home and said, 'Dear Ma, Yi, yi, yi, yi, yi. Love, Papa.' "

* * *

"Even in the worst of dilemmas, there is usually some one thing that we can do. We are never so woe begone that we are completely unable to do anything at all. I am reminded of traveling in Nigeria in a Ford pick-up. Out there, being under British influence, we turn to the left and drive improperly on the left side of the highway. And one day as I was rounding a blind curve, driving on a middle-of-the-road policy, there suddenly appeared before me another Ford pick-up going in the opposite direction and following the same middle-of-the-road policy. Now as you may surmise, something had to be done. Under the stress of the situation, I reverted to my childhood pattern of behavior and turned to the right side of the road, which was wrong. Fortunately, the other car was also driven by an American, and he reverted and turned to the right, which really was all that was left. From a moral and legal point of view, we were both mistaken, but as I said, there is usually something that can be done that gets us through the pinch of the dilemma."

* * *

"My uncle Rufus Bucher had a hired man who helped him cutting corn one year. They went out at ten o'clock in the morning; it was still frosty and chilly and they sat on the stake and rider fence, waiting for it to get warmer still. But it didn't seem to pay off, and Uncle Rufus decided we better get at it since it won't get better. So they started down the field and back again, flailing about with their corn knives, until they had finished the whole field, and they came back and sat down on the same fence at the same place. Uncle Rufus said to the hired man— to the hired man, mind you—'How do you feel now?' And the hired man said, 'I wish there were more corn.' And that's the way it is in the Christian life. We solve a lot of our problems by disregarding them and just pressing on under the prize of the high calling of God in Christ Jesus."

* * *

"A hundred men were assigned to hold an air dirigible in San Diego, Calif. At a signal all were to let go. Two persons didn't. As they were pulled up, one let go and fell to his death. The other held on until finally he was rescued. A faith is not a ladder which we erect on our own experience. It is a rope by which we·hang from God."

* * *

In talking about unsuccessful relationships, William shared this interchange:

Man (handing ring to the woman) "I hand this ring to you as a symbol of my love—it has no end."

Woman (handing ring back to the man) "I return this ring to you as a symbol of my love—it has no beginning."

* * *

'When Sherlock Holmes arrived in heaven, St. Peter asked for identification and Sherlock said he didn't have any. St. Peter said, "How do we know it's you." "Give me a task in identification," Sherlock replied. "I'm famous for that kind of thing." St. Peter agreed, and promptly took him to a room where there were one hundred people, all of them with no clothes on. "Tell me which is Adam and which is Eve," St. Peter challenged. Sherlock looked around a little bit and said, "There is Adam and over there is Eve." St. Peter was puzzled. "How did you do that so fast?" "Elementary," Sherlock responded, "no belly buttons." '

* * *

"I remember in 1911 living in Virginia. Brother Galen B. Royer came down there, looking for eleven good men to send to the mission field. He got one of them, took my grammar teacher and sent him as a missionary to Sweden, and I've been handicapped ever since."

* * *

On the nature of forgiving love as revealed in the cross, he said, "Here is a man who decides to confess everything to his wife by telling her of his unfaithfulness. If the wife would say, 'Think nothing of it, George,' then there would really be no genuine forgiveness. Genuine forgiveness always involves judgment. On the other hand, if the wife would refuse to speak at all and have nothing to do with him from that point on, you would have the judgment without any forgiveness. True forgiveness only comes in the context of judgment."

* * *

"I remember riding some years ago through the parched areas of northeastern Nigeria. The day was longer than we had anticipated, and we had less drinking water along than we needed. We stopped to visit a local chieftain thinking he might give us some gingerale. But what he had was not acceptable to us as honorary members of the W.C.T.U. The best he could do instead was to bring us out some gumdrops and some dry cookies of biscuits opened from a tin, and the requirements of hospitality and guesthood dried us up and left us in a powder. We still had eighteen miles to drive toward home and you could have spun yarn out of the cotton in our mouths. As we got out of the jeep and began unloading our gear, here under the seat where Leland Brubaker and I were sitting were two canteens of the juiciest kind of drinking water waiting for our participation. Now there was a big difference between having it under the seat and having it in the mouth. The surpassing worth of knowing and participating in Jesus Christ as Lord is my major concern."

* * *

Looking around over an adult camp in Iowa-Minnesota, he said, "Since this is an adult audience, I think it will be all right to tell this story. There were two Scotchmen. They were a pair of tights."

* * *

"I remember the story of an Episcopal Bishop in New York. When he went to Albany, he signed all his letters, William of Albany, and later he got bolder and signed, William Albany. One of his classmates said, 'You better stop that. They may move you to Buffalo and call you Buffalo Bill.' "

* * *

Note on a program from a speech he heard: "It was so dry in the

South—the Brethren were doing single immersion, the Baptists were using sprinkling, the Presbyterians went to a damp washcloth, and the Methodists were giving a raincheck."

* * *

On the decline of the missionary hymn, "From Greenland's Icy Mountains," and related missionary zeal, he said, "The aspect of the 19th century climate which has perhaps led us to this is the sense of superiority which we arrogated to ourselves because of the advantages which were ours. On the obverse side this took the form of pity, condescension, or even disdain for those less favored. The raw edge of this snobbery attached itself to words like 'heathen,' 'native,' 'pagan,' and it led to such phrases as the 'unspeakable Turk,' 'followers of the false prophet,' and such doggerel as:
'The poor deluded Hindu,
He tries the best he can do;
He sticks to caste
From first to last;
For clothes he makes his skin do.' "

* * *

Speaking in Bethany Seminary Chapel just before leaving for Nigeria he noted his subject would be sheep, and his remarks would be based on four points. The first, black sheep; the second, white sheep; the third, hydraulic ram; and the fourth, Mary's little lamb. As the talk developed, the black sheep were the Africans to whom the gospel was being taken, the white sheep were the missionary families they would visit, the hydraulic ram was the airplane which would transport the whole party to Nigeria, and Mary's little lamb was the One in whose name it was all being done.

* * *

"There is the story of the ram who ran off the edge of the cliff and plunged to his death. . . . . because he didn't see the ewe turn."

* * *

"One of the great joys of life is to move from acknowledgement to participation, and one of the great tragedies of life is to move to acknowledgement and stop short of participation."

A missionary from another denomination whom William knew was a visiting chapel speaker at Bethany Seminary. After the man left, William shared a story about him. When the man first arrived on the mission field, he fretted because he was spending most of his time in language studies and wasn't getting any missionary work done. Since he wanted to be doing something else and since he had done some dynamiting on the farm, he was given the job of setting off a charge of dynamite to blast loose some large tree stumps from the new right-of-way for the road. Because it was the custom of the natives to take a siesta over the hot noon hour, he got everything in readiness one noon and lit the fuse. To his horror, he saw a native woman walking down the path toward the dynamite. Unable to speak the language to her, he shouted in English, beckoned and waved frantically, but she kept on her way. To prevent her from being blown to bits, he ran and grabbed her, throwing her to the ground on the safe side of a large stump covering her with his body, as he waited for the charge to go off. It never exploded! William noted that the man had a hard time living that one down, and he fussed less about the language after that.

* * *

"There was this Pennsylvania brother who went 300 miles to Annual Meeting at Philadelphia. He wrote home to his wife and said, 'Dear Ma, If the world goes as far on the other side as it does this way, it must be quite a place.' "

* * *

Complete Text of Talk Given in Bethany Chapel 1948

"It is conceivable that there might someday appear a few lines in the 'Gains for the Kingdom' column of the Gospel Messenger reporting Holy Week Services at Greensburg, Pennsylvania, with 46 accessions to the church, mostly by baptism and a few by letter. Unless there is care, there might even be added Evangelist, William M. Beahm of Bethany Biblical Seminary, Chicago. If you ever see such a statement, view it with caution. You may believe that I was a visiting minister and attempted to set forth a week's worth of evangelistic messages. You may believe, likewise, that there were 46 bona fide accessions to the church, mostly by baptism of the three-dip, clear-under variety which got them wet enough they knew something was going on. You may believe there was joy on heaven and on earth when these came forward on stated occasions to declare their intentions as well as when they walked out of the water into the enfolding fellowship of the church.

But if you are tempted to infer that the visiting evangelist wrought such wonders, don't yield. I was in the Spirit. And I did put forth considerable effort. But there was plenty of evidence every day that such results were the effect of the sustained and persuasive efforts of the Prince of Brethren Evangelists, Mahlon J. Brougher. I was there all right. But it was all I could do not to retard the pace or hinder the passion with which he was seeking the lost. I was reminded of the boy's idea of the function of a rabbit's front feet. 'It is the business of a rabbit's front feet to keep out of the way of his hind feet as they do the jumping.'

I wish therefore to report on Greensburg, not for what I did but for what I saw being done. Perhaps the happiest experience of the week was the baptism of the whole Bell family, with their four children. . . . We called on Wednesday or Thursday, but only the mother was at home. She doubted if we could ever see them all at once. But by grace and patience, she agreed we might come back on Saturday at 4:00. There in the disrupted living room we had a great experience. The furniture was removed and they had been sanding the floor and puttying the cracks. We stood around the edges—six Bells and two visiting ministers.

The issue was soon raised—would the boys become Christians tomorrow on Easter? After a while the second one agreed, but the oldest one demurred. Presently, the six-year old boy said he wanted to. Then the eleven-year old girl agreed eagerly. Finally, the oldest boy overcame his shyness and joined in the great choice. Brother Brougher then turned to father Bell and invited him as well. He said they just as well make it a family affair and urged mother Bell to join in, too.

We left that hallowed home with the ship's call in our hearts. Six Bells and all's well! The next morning they were baptized in Brother Brougher's quiet, devout and impressive fashion. Each stood in the baptistry until the whole redeemed family stood there together and marched out into the new life as a unit. Talk about ringing bells, that did. I learned that merchants in the town had offered great services to triplets and greater ones to quadruplets just born. Here were sextuplets reborn!

Baptism is not something to argue about, it is something to administer. I hope many of you can approximate Brother Brougher's skill. With 46 baptisms, there were 168 immersions or dips and I heard only one slight cough!

I could probably find some mistakes in this 37-year career of (M. J. Brougher). There would likely be some limitations and difficulties in the picture. All I can say is that I'd be glad to have any of us go out and show these same limitations and make these same mistakes if we could at the same time prove so effective in our ministry in the building of a local church.

My talk is not an argument nor a contingent today. I am merely reporting on Holy Week at Greensburg, Pa., 1948. I am like the rooster who brought an ostrich egg and set it in the henyard, saying 'I'm not entering a complaint. I am showing you what is being done in some other places!' "

* * *

From a Marriage Service, December 1952

To the bride and groom:

If you wish your new estate to be touched with perennial beauty, cherish those gracious visions which have made spring within your hearts during the days of your betrothal. You must never forget nor deny the vision you once saw; you must resolve that it be not blotted out nor blurred by the commonplace experiences of life. Faults may appear which were once hidden in a golden mist; excellencies may seem to fade in the glare of the noon-day sun. Still be unmoved in your devotion; still hopeful — amid the reality of present imperfection, believe in the ideal. You saw it once — it still exists — it is final truth — you are performing an act of utter faith. This is the man, that is the woman you love. That is the shape of spiritual beauty God sees and which for an hour he showed to you. That is the soul which is to be when this conflict with temptations, hindrances, and failure is accomplished. Hide that image in your inmost heart. Make real this ideal in your united lives and your home will be a place of repair and harbour, a dwelling place of contentment and abiding joy.

* * *

On an Office Memorandum Note — An Introduction of Morley Mays, a Past President of Elizabethtown College

I did not have the privilege of knowing Morley Mays in our unregenerate days, and therefore I have neither the shame nor the nostalgic relish of remembering our early times together.

For nearly 20 years now I have counted him as a friend beyond my deserving, and of great reward to me through campus bull sessions at the University of Chicago, in conversations and visits at Bridgewater and Juniata College, and in the hospitality of their home. I am in deep debt to him and Mrs. Mays.

He is one who has deeply discerned the winds of doctrine and tides of thought which play upon us and our Christian faith. He is one who grapples creatively and trustworthily with the issues confronting our faith. We delight in the leads he gives us in bringing the resources of our faith to bear on the issues of our time.

* * *

On the Back of a Letter, a Handwritten Introduction dated Thurs. Nov. 2, 9:40 A.M.

We have come to the end of the 1961 E.B. Hoff Lecture series. As for an introduction, all we need to say is "that man is here again." As we face their ending we do it with sweet sorrow . . . Looking back over what has happened here this week in a delightful acquaintance with a man who has labored in the vineyard for a quarter century unknown to us. In the last decade, however, his books have left us with a shock of glory as they shared the wealth of his concern for the life of the Spirit in the Soul and in the Church. Then waves of his speaking ministry came to us echoing now here and now there. And at long last now the man himself has endeared himself to us by his virile dignity, and disarming simplicity and friendliness. We have been enriched, disrupted, and lifted as he has opened up to us the raucous abyss of our technological culture and also the robust webs of healing strength which comes to us from God in Christian Worship. For long in the future we can recall this week's encounter as a pattern of what things should be said about the center of man's need for redemption, the center of the Christian Gospel, and a pattern of how these things should be said for effective communication.

Dr. Samuel H. Miller — We thank you and wish you God's continued favor on your work. You have blessed us — Do it once more on the topic, "The Disciplines of the Spirit."

* * *

From a Lecture to His Seminary Students

"When we try to validate the Gospel on the basis of the world's standards, we are in grave trouble indeed. People like to validate the Gospel because the Gospel is relevant to the modern day, and so we go at it the way others do. Do you get dizzy? Are you easily dazed? Are you easily excited? Do your hands tremble? Does your heart flutter? Are you easily irritated? Try Lepsog. Are you easily frightened? Is your temper irritable? Is your sleep unrefreshing? Do you suffer from neuralgia? Is there a twitching of the muscle? Do you forget what you read? Do you have a languid feeling? Try Lepsog. And spell it backwards and you have Gospel. And we feel we really have the revealed word of God straight from heaven because it is relevant to this list which I copied from a patent medicine advertisement. Now I hope you understand me. I think the gospel is relevant to these, but the point is the norms and standards of our Gospel are simply out of this world. And we must keep this clear."

CHAPTER FIVE

"Hurt to Hurt Talk . . . "

1960 was a hard year for William. A note from his physician, Dr. Gonzales says that in January of that year he underwent an initial examination which did not indicate a serious problem. But by June, minor prostate surgery was performed, again with good results and with the pathologist's report indicating no evidence of malignancy. But as the year progressed, a growth appeared and began to enlarge. Dr. Gonzales' note of December 15 indicates William was put on medication and informed that major surgery for malignancy was required.

The four years between the surgery and his death in 1964 included two more years as dean at Bethany Seminary; after his retirement a part of the third year teaching at Bridgewater College; and a final time in retirement at Boulder Hill, Illinois. The four years were days of battle with cancer. They were days of adjustment, days of pain, days of courage. Though he seldom during that time knew "surcease" from pain, he managed most of the four years to retain the twinkle, the careful word, the flash of humor, the love of the way a thing was said.

An additional pain to his bodily suffering, and one which he found harder to be gracious about, was the pain of well-meaning friends who were writing him and telling him that if he had enough faith, he could get well.

He made no effort to hide his malignancy, nor did he withdraw from talking about it or sharing his struggles. He gravitated toward others who were in pain or were caught up in a life and death struggle, finding comfort in sharing physical and faith experiences with them. It was during this time that what had been a somewhat cool and casual relationship with Kermit Eby, professor at the University of Chicago and also fighting cancer, grew into a very close and meaningful friendship. I often took William to see Kermit, listened to them do battle with the "demon" within them, and heard them inspect and celebrate the faith that was important to them.

"Hurt to hurt talk . . . " includes stories and sayings from this four year period. And since the portrait began with words about William, it ends with words about him. There are several letters, and the sermon preached at his memorial service.

After his first operation for malignancy, I went to the hospital, wondering what I as a pastor could say to this man who seemed always to say the right things to me. As I walked in the room, he looked up from amongst the I.V.'s and catheter hoses and said, with a feeble smile, "Earle, be thankful when your plumbing works."

* * *

In the early stages of William's illness, before it was known that his condition was terminal, a friend asked how he was doing. He responded, "I am doing fairly well, and the doctors have told me that I will probably die of some other cause before what I have takes me. That pleased me," he said, "until I stopped to think about it."

* * *

Sometimes William was very blunt. During the last Annual Conference which he attended, when people took his hand to shake it and said, "How are you, Brother," he responded directly, "Dying."

* * *

William brought apple logs from his tree in his Villa Park back yard to the Harold Row's fireplace on Hubbard Avenue in Elgin. The fire was crackling and burning brightly and he drew up a chair and said to Leona, who was just recovering from hepatitis, "I sense that people are enjoying the morsels about our ill health."

* * *

"All the problems of old age seem to add up to having your money, your health, and your spouse come out even."

* * *

He was aware that his sharing of the pains and concerns about his illness sometimes bothered persons. He would say, "Guess you're tired of my bellyaching."

* * *

When William was recuperating from his operation, I went in to see him one day and said, as I entered the door, "How are you this day, Brother William?" He looked at me and said, "I know what the resurrection is. Today is my first day without the hot iron of pain in six weeks."

* * *

Just before his death William was visited by Ernest Snell. Both men were small in stature. William called him the little deacon. Mr. Snell had just had a severe heart attack and was suffering from glaucoma. After an hour's visit, they shook hands and kissed one another goodbye. William looked up and said, "Ernie, I sure enjoyed this hurt-to-hurt talk."

* * *

During his hopsital convalescence, he was resting one day when a knock came on the door. A nurse entered, and she proceeded to give him a bath, a "wash all over" as William called it. When she had finished and was just about to go out the door, he said, "Nurse, I have a question. Why did you bother to knock?"

* * *

One of the treatments for William's prostate malignancy was to take hormones. The first one prescribed created a reaction which caused him to break out in a rash all over his body. It was a frightening experience. But worse than the fear was the itching. When the doctor came in, he said, "Doc, you got to give me something for this rash. Now I don't want something to take it away, it's too much fun to scratch. Just give me something to save the skin."

* * *

Several weeks before William died, he talked with his sister, Anna. "How will it be," he said, "when I cross over?"

* * *

Letters

From Kermit Eby to William, dated February 19, 1962

Dear Brother Bill,

To one who moved my heart with prayer as it has never been moved before;
Anytime you want to come see me, please do so.

Sincerely,

Kermit

* * *

From Kermit Eby to William, dated April 22, 1962

Dear Bill,

For some time I have been wanting to put in words what your visits meant to me. Yours was an amazing presence. You gave me faith and strength. And one sentence you gave me: "You and I are living in two worlds."

* * *

From a letter dated August 14, 1963 from Dr. Andrew Cordier, Dean, Columbia University

You have been in the thoughts and prayers of Dorothy and myself for many months. . . . As I walked with Dag Hammarskjold at 4:00 o'clock one morning in the midst of great crisis, we looked to the starry heavens and he said, "The twinkle of that star is the span of our life in the long expanse of time which reaches into eternity." This twinkle perhaps varies a bit for members of the human family, but it proves again that it is not the length of our years but what we have done with them that counts.

Your life has been profoundly rich in a continuous flow of rich blessings to humanity. Many thousands of people have been inspired to a better life through your resourceful teaching and your fine Christian example.

We hope that the healing powers of nature, the resourcefulness of medicine, and the deep faith that you possess in God and things eternal may prolong your life. Your many friends everywhere are praying for your recovery. May God bless and keep you. Faithfully, Andrew.

* * *

Funeral Sermon for William M. Beahm

by Earle W. Fike, Jr.
April 15, 1964

Tucked away in the fifth chapter of Genesis is a genealogy, very repetitious and uninspiring in its account of certain lives. Nine times we are told how long a certain man lived, the number of children, and nine times the account closes with the words "and he died." But there, shining like some precious stone in the hodge-podge of an ordinary notions counter is this sentence: "Enoch walked with God, and was not, for God took him." There was something special about Enoch. His closeness with God made a difference in his life and his death.

There was something special about William Beahm. No man walks with God without being different. But he was more different than the average. Closeness to God means a deeper closeness to all men. Closeness to Christ means that no decision is easy or unimportant before Him who is the way; no contented or atrophied intellect is permissible before Him who is the Truth; no uninvolved spectator living is possible in the presence of Him who is the Life. No one walks with God without having some special place in an otherwise ordinary genealogy.

As Christians, we stand in an unusual heritage. "See what love the Father has given us, that we should be called children of God; and so we are. The reason why the world does not know us is that it did not know him. Beloved, we are God's children now; it does not yet appear what we shall be, but we know that when he appears, we shall be like him, for we shall see him as he is." That's an open-ended genealogy which makes Enoch's experience of closeness to God for eternity available to all of us. Yet within this unusual genealogy, and because of it, there are special people. And there was something special about William Beahm.

In this he was special: no man I have known has known more people — called them by name — their middle name — and eight times out of ten, their mother's maiden name. The genealogy of a person was important to our brother, I'm convinced not just as a mental exercise for an agile mind, but more in the sense of the scriptural importance of genealogies.

In the Bible, it is of paramount importance to know who you are, and to do this you must know from whence you came and to whom you belong. Brother William knew to whom he belonged, whose he was, and therefore he knew the One to whom all rightly belong. In his words, everyone is a person "for whom Christ died." But because Brother William was special and had to do things deeply, that general truth wasn't enough. Every person was a particular child of God and needed to be known specifically and individually. If Bro. Beahm knew you, you couldn't say, as James Baldwin says bitterly in the title of his novel, "Nobody Knows My Name." The kind of individual care which our brother found as he walked with God rubbed off in his care for others.

In this way also, he was special; the full spectrum of life's experiences were fascinating and meaningful to him. There was little that happened to him which escaped intense investigation. He entered into life deeply.

This quality nurtured his keen humor. For only one who has plumbed the deepest of life with understanding can add to the joy and fun of life with freedom and sensitivity. Only one who knows life dares frivolity. Indeed was not Christ himself a master of the simple and the clever — the profound and the pun?

But this same quality made his suffering more intense and his release more gratifying. The mental pain of first knowing his condition; the spiritual pain of being reconciled to it; and the physical pain which his condition finally forced upon him were all subject to the same intense investigation which marked his manner of living. And even as he shared the agonies of that struggle, so he shared the joys of that first day without the "hot iron within him." He suffered greatly, he rejoiced freely, he questioned profoundly, and he believed deeply. But because of his specialness, we must question whether we really know the depths or heights of any of these experiences. We know only that the destructive force within his body never contaminated his spirit.

This quality of eager participation encouraged him toward openness of mind, but also bound him to sturdiness of conviction. In his years as teacher, the winds of theology blew strong in many directions, and he was conversant with them. But within that flexibility there was a sturdiness on basic doctrine which provided a rock upon which his ministry could be built.

This quality of intense involvement must surely have stayed with him in these last days. I can only see him deeply engaged in the process of death and different life; pausing here and there, unhurried, savoring, testing, contemplating, piecing together in his careful way the full glory of that experience.

What I have tried to say is this: within any genealogy, there are those who stand out significantly. Enoch did in an otherwise colorless family tree. We stand in a far greater lineage as children of God through Jesus Christ. But even within that genealogy there are those who are distinct. I would not seek to canonize Brother Beahm, for there is something in him which most would like to be — something of wholeness and sturdiness and kindness. Something of attractive depth. Something of a twinkle — and a tear. Something very special.

Date Due

May 10			